Direct Encounter

Direct Encounter

A lifetime adventure

Joyce Mitchell

CASTLE PUBLISHING
AUCKLAND
NEW ZEALAND

Direct Encounter
Published by Castle Publishing Ltd
PO Box 68-800 Newton,
Auckland, New Zealand
Phone: +64-9-378 4052
Fax: +64-9-376 3855

© 2000 Joyce Mitchell

ISBN 0-9582124-5-7

Part One was first published in 1963, as
'A Practical Housewife's Approach to Christ',
by Challenge Publications.
Part Two was first published in 1968, as
'A Practical Housewife's Involvement with Christ',
by the author.
Text revised and rewritten for this edition.

Cover design and layout by Jeff Hagan
Printed in New Zealand by Wentforth Print

CONTENTS

Foreword

The evening had ended. The lights had been turned out in the church hall where our women's group met. My friend and I stood outside chatting, almost hesitant to go home and lose the impact of the evening.

'I'd like to be like that!' I said to my friend.

'So would I,' she agreed.

It was the first time I had heard Joyce Mitchell speak. She had shared with us her experience of God and something in us had responded to her obvious joy. It drew out of us a previously unspoken longing. This was a crucial step in my own journey.

In those early years of the seventies there must have been many women like me who responded to Joyce's testimony and ministry as she spoke to groups across Auckland.

It was with great pleasure that I saw again the cover of her little book and learned that it, together with her two other works, is to be republished as one volume.

I pray that the Lord she loves will bless this new edition of Joyce Mitchell's writing, and that it will bring light and encouragement to all who read it.

CAROLYN KILLICK

Acknowledgements

I wish to express my appreciation for the work Grace and Trevor Shaw and Joy Dawson did checking the original manuscripts of my first two books. To my friends of those days, Constance Deane, Rev. J. A. Gunn, and to Max McLachlan for his riptide story.

To John Massam and Andrew Killick of Castle Publishing for their work on this new revised edition. To Carolyn Killick, Stewart Hillman, Carolyn Killick and Kay Wall for their editing and proofreading.

To my husband John and daughters Gail and Christine for the patience and acceptance that they showed. And to God who gave me my abundant life.

PART ONE

APPROACH TO GOD

1

The Adventuresome Years

Although my father died when I was only four years old, my childhood in Auckland, New Zealand was one of happiness and security. My mother was left with four children - three girls and a boy, two under the age of five. She was strong, healthy and very capable.

We could rely on Mum. She was always there when we came home from school and she never went out at night - we were her life.

When I was sixteen I became a member of the local Presbyterian church in Mt. Albert. I attended quite regularly and took Communion. Both my brother and sister were members and I guess I thought it was the right thing to do.

When I was eighteen, a strange thing happened. I was at home one day, when suddenly I heard a strong voice inside me say, 'Follow me.' I was shaken by this unusual experience. Somehow I knew it was the voice of God, but my natural response was to say, 'No - there's so much out there in the world that I want to find out about.' Christianity wasn't very attractive from what I could see. It was governed by laws that stated, 'Thou shalt not'. I knew that it was impossible for me to keep those laws. I understood that if I broke one, I broke the lot. Instead of responding to the voice, I decided to set out to live a good life, do noble things and try to work my way into heaven.

Life was on the up and up for me. I had the good fortune to obtain a position, as an accountant, in a large wine and spirit wholesale firm.

The salary was well above that of girls my own age and, consequently, I became very interested in clothes. This position and its responsibility inflated my ego.

Gradually the excitement, pleasures and opportunities to do things my own way, crowded out my spiritual life. I had mentally assented to Christ in the past, but now I stopped going to church and threw away Christianity.

Like most girls of nineteen I was romantic. The lure of overseas places was fascinating. Wonderful coloured pictures of the Islands with blue sea, white sand and overhanging palm trees awakened in me the urge to travel and see these places for myself.

Through careful saving and planning I went first on a South Pacific Island cruise, then on a trip with Mum to Australia. Although these were wonderful experiences, there was one thing that took some of the glamour away. I was a terrible sailor. As long as the ship was in motion I was confined to my cabin. I also found out that there are two kinds of seasick people - those who're afraid they are going to die, and those who're afraid they are not going to die. I was in the latter category.

After this experience with ships, I was quite convinced that I was not a sailor and that for all future travel I would go by air.

Around this time I discovered golf. My friend Julia told me about her cousin and his friend who had recently opened a men's clothing and sports store in downtown Auckland. So off I went to buy my new clubs. When I arrived at the shop, the first thing I noticed was her cousin's friend - a big tall guy with auburn hair and the loveliest blue eyes I'd ever seen - John Mitchell. He didn't have to persuade me to buy the clubs! I was sold as soon as I saw him.

About two weeks later another friend of mine, at Middlemore Golf Club, told me that John wanted to take me to the annual ball but was too shy to ask. Nervously, I told him that I would go with John. I'll never forget that night when our romance began.

John had worked for six months, at the Westfield Freezing Works, to raise capital to start his business. About six months after it opened, his partner decide to pull out. I advised him to buy his partner's share and said that I would help him in the business as much as I could.

One day after work, when I went to his shop, John produced a ring and told me he wanted to marry me. I was so excited and couldn't get home fast enough to tell Mum the news.

We announced our engagement in June 1938. Then, in September 1939, came the terrible news of war. In our happy surroundings, this came as a bomb in itself. One by one the boys were called up, leaving an emptiness that would not be filled. Time became very precious and life took on greater momentum as we tried to live a lifetime in the few months we had left together.

John was all I had ever dreamed of in a man. We made wonderful plans together but we knew that we would have to wait to be married. John wanted to join Scheme B in the Navy; this meant that he would go to England as a civilian and train to be an officer in the Royal Navy. Marriage would make him ineligible. So he left for England and began training at the Gunnery School at Lowestoft on the east coast, north of London. His training included time at sea, as a gunner on a destroyer, escorting supply convoys to Murmansk in Russia.

He then transferred to another destroyer, HMS *Trinidad*. Its role was to cover the back of the convoy and protect it from German submarines hoping to pick off the slow ships that couldn't hold their place. On one escort the officers aboard *Trinidad* spotted a torpedo coming towards them. It struck amidships and disabled the vessel. Orders stood that no ship was to stop to pick up survivors from any disabled ship, but another destroyer broke orders, came alongside and allowed those on *Trinidad*'s decks to jump aboard. John was one of the lucky ones.

15

John was eventually commissioned as a lieutenant and given command of a 'submarine chaser' of the Fairmile class. He was required to go out in dangerous weather with winds exceeding gale force. On the Russian convoys there were times when the weather was so cold that the guns froze and couldn't be fired. He told us that his worst experience of the war was the occasion when on gunnery practice he missed the target and instead hit the boat towing it. He was sick with worry while he waited to be dressed down by the 'big brass'. Yet, through all his naval experiences, John was developing a life-long love of the sea.

When John first decided to enlist we had to consider what was to happen with his store. These were uncertain times and I could have been called up for service as well. We discussed the problem with Mum, who said, 'You must keep those doors open whatever happens. When all the men come back from the war you'll make a fortune in men's clothing.' I tried to be released from my job, but with all the male staff leaving, the firm couldn't spare me. So with the help of two girls we pressed on with the goal of keeping John's business open. As menswear was almost at a standstill, we branched into other lines, and life became very busy as I worked hard to hold both jobs.

There are twenty-four hours in a day and I used every minute of them. My weekends were spent playing golf. Enthusiasm for golf is sometimes termed as a disease and there was no doubt that I had caught the bug. I had a lesson twice a week and used to get up early in the morning and practise my swing before I went to work. Any free time at night I spent 'putting' on the carpet. Within five years my handicap was down to six.

I was now a club champion and had the honour of representing my club in the annual 'Champion of Champions' tournamant. I was soon lured into amateur tournament golf, touring golf courses throughout the North Island of New Zealand.

Always with an eye to business, I became golf clothes conscious. The male members dwindled but women were still playing, so I concentrated on wet weather clothes, hats and blouses. Wearing and promoting these clothes myself, the project flourished.

Golf only took second place in the months of August and September, when the call of the pure white snow at Mt. Ruapehu couldn't be denied. I belonged to an enthusiastic ski club, and when the secretary was called up for overseas duty I filled the position. During these months a party of about forty of us would take our annual vacation and spend two weeks at the Chateau Tongariro, a winter resort on the central plateau of the North Island. Here we held our highly competitive winter sports events. After a few years I became 'Lady Champion' of the club.

Skiing was becoming very popular now and our club was the first to have a ski tow. People were demanding ski pants, parkas, ski hats, boots, gloves and socks. As Ski Club secretary, I had no choice but to fulfil these demands, and so business flourished even more.

These were adventuresome years and we had some wonderful South Island skiing trips to Mt. Cook, the Tasman Glacier and Coronet Peak, where the snow was comparable with the best ski fields overseas.

Although the ski season is quite short in New Zealand, we crammed in as much as we could. There were times when we would get up early in Auckland, have a quick breakfast of bacon and eggs, take on the six hour trip to Mt. Ruapehu and be skiing by ten o'clock the same morning.

There was still more to the social side of my life. During the war my brother spent time in Canada, America and England. Both he and John wrote home with glowing reports of the hospitality extended to the Forces overseas in these countries.

How wonderful it was, they wrote, to spend an evening by the fireside in a private home or to eat a home-cooked meal; to have somebody interested in your well-being and to know that when you were fed up with barracks, a soft armchair was always waiting for you.

By now the American troops were stationed in New Zealand and the boys had heard of this and asked us to do whatever we could to return the hospitality. A social whirl developed and many, many nights were spent in dining and dancing.

As the years went on, schoolboys turned into young men. They would come into the shop to buy sport shirts, which were in short supply. Stocks were scarce in all the stores. Most of the factories were under contract to the Government to make uniforms.

I toyed with the idea of making sport shirts myself and bought a couple of bolts of material with some patterns. One night Mum and I sat on the floor and cut out two dozen shirts. I placed an advertisement in the paper and employed women to sew them in their own homes. Another lady buttonholed and sewed on buttons. Finally I collected the shirts, took them home, pressed them and took them to the shop to sell. They sold like hot cakes. Big things always start from little beginnings, but little did I know that a manufacturing business would spring from two dozen shirts cut out on the floor at home.

For four years John was away in England serving with the Navy. One day I received the wonderful news that he was coming back on six months leave. We decided to be married while he was home. In tense excitement, family and friends helped prepare for the wedding. It was just the kind of wedding that a girl during the war dreamed of - a white wedding with all the men in naval officers' uniforms.

John wasn't only big in stature, six feet three and a-half inches tall, but he also thought big. Together we planned to make shirts and more shirts. We made an ideal business couple, for as he planned I handled the financial details of the business. Peace was declared before the year was up, so John never returned to England.

John and Joyce Mitchell were married in 1945

Just as Mum had predicted, the boys came back from overseas looking for new clothes to replace their uniforms, and we were ready for them.

For the first years of our marriage we lived in the upper storey of John's parents' big home in Epsom, one of Auckland's most established suburbs. My sister and her husband were looking for a section and we went with them to Titirangi. The moment we saw the sections we fell in love with the view. Titirangi is situated on the foothills of the Waitakere Ranges which are covered with beautiful native bush. We purchased three joining sections across the slopping site for ourselves and finished building the house after eighteen months.

Our unique ninety-degree view took in the beautiful Waitemata Harbour flowing into the Pacific Ocean on the left. On the right was the Manukau Harbour, with its tidal shadows and huge sandbars, into which flows the Tasman Sea. The centre view was of the Auckland area with its many small mountains bobbing up here and there. We were only five minutes away from one of the most picturesque golf courses in New Zealand.

Business thrived. By this time we owned a shop, a factory, a home, a car each, and a dog each. Then in a few more years our lovely daughters, Gail and Christine, were born. Later we added a beach house to our possessions. People admired us for the success we had made of our lives. But all this time God was working behind the scenes.

I understood how to take stock of a balance sheet. However, one day I started to take stock of my life. I realised that I had been taking out of life far more than I had been putting back in, and now I felt a terrific emptiness in me. I had everything a person could want, but still I was dissatisfied. I came face to face with the real meaning of the verse in the Bible that says,

'What good is it for a man to gain the whole world, yet forfeit his soul?' Mark 8:36.

The Mitchell home in Titirangi

2

A Sudden Awakening

One day I went onto the balcony of our beautiful home and looked up at the clear blue sky. I remember saying to myself, 'There's a God up there, but I don't know him.'

I had always called myself a Christian. I believed in God because right from early childhood I had been told there was a God - creator of heaven and earth and everything in it. But somehow just believing didn't seem to be satisfactory.

Sometimes, when the mood took me, I would read my Bible. After reading one night, I decided I wanted to get to know God on a personal level. From then on the Bible seemed to take on a different meaning, a new look. I found verses that showed what I desired was there for me if I wanted it.

'Come to me, all you who are weary and burdened, and I will give you rest.' Matthew 11:28.

'All that the Father gives me will come to me, and whoever comes to me I will never drive away.' John 6:37.

'Seek and you will find.' Luke 11:9.

One verse that really impressed me contained Jesus' words to his disciples about the 'kingdom of God',

> *'No one can see the kingdom of God unless he is born again. No one can enter the kingdom of God unless he is born of water and the Spirit.'* John 3:3,5.

These verses were a mystery to me, but by this time I had set my heart on pursuing the kingdom. I didn't know exactly what or where this kingdom was, but I knew that was where I wanted to be. One afternoon I went into my bedroom, got on my knees and prayed as I had never prayed before; believing that if I went to God and asked him, he would show me the way.

A few nights later in bed, my prayer was answered. I dreamed a dream so vivid I can still see it today. I saw Christ on the cross, blood flowing from his wounds. I was there asking why the innocent Christ should suffer for me. I heard him say, 'So you may see the kingdom of God.' Again I got down on my knees. I begged his forgiveness and repented with all my heart.

That same night I had another dream. Before me were two faces, one evil and the other beautiful, calm and peaceful. They seemed to be having words about me, then they turned and the evil face said, 'I will give you all the things of the world.'

The other said, 'I will give you eternal life.'

Then a voice boomed out, 'CHOOSE.'

I knew that I had to make the decision immediately. I couldn't put it off or have time to think about it. I felt it would be my last chance; my mind flashed back to when I was eighteen and had turned my back on God. Now, with this sense of urgency, I chose to go with Christ and choose eternal life.

I had a feeling as if I wasn't alone in the room but I was too scared to open my eyes. I felt the bed go down as if someone had sat on it and a wisp of something that could have been a slight breeze passed over my forehead. From that moment my fears vanished and all was calm. I was conscious of God. I didn't have to guess what it was all about. I knew God had put out his hand and I had taken it.

A few days later my minister rang and asked if I would take a 'Bible in Schools' class. I was so surprised. I had prayed that God would show me what to do next, but I had never done anything like that in my life before, as I was quick to tell my minister. The children loomed before me in the shape of some prehistoric monster with forty small heads and each one was grimacing at me.

'Oh no, not for me, I'm not going to get caught in this one,' I thought.

I was just on the point of refusing when the prayer that I had said, 'God show me what you want me to do', came ringing back in my ears. 'This is it,' I thought, 'he wants me to serve him.' To my minister's astonishment, after all my protestations, I suddenly said that I would try.

The following Thursday morning I went off, still with the 'monster' in my mind. I was terrified, but I asked Christ to help. When I started the lesson I couldn't believe it was me; Christ's strength lifted me up and I found that working with children was amazingly satisfying.

After a few more weeks, while doing my housework, I became conscious of the fact that I must be baptised. I kept telling myself that it wasn't really necessary for salvation, but deep down I knew that something had to be done.

I hadn't been baptised as a baby so when I approached my minister he was most willing to arrange it, until I said that nothing less than total immersion would do. I thought that I had better confide in him about my 'experience'. I wanted to help him understand why I was asking for immersion, when the doctrine of our church says that immersion is not necessary and that a sprinkle or pouring will suffice.

After six month's waiting he arranged to use another church's baptismal pool, explaining to their minister, 'Joyce Mitchell's got a bee in her bonnet!'

On the 10th November 1958 I was baptised by total immersion, by my own minister, with members of my church attending. I completely understood that the symbol of my baptism was a going down into death with Christ and arising in new life. It was an experience I will never forget. An immense surge of strength filled me. As I surrendered my heart, will, mind and body to God, my life seemed to pour out and I was like an empty container.

The peace and calm that followed was wonderful. I knew with assurance that God had my life in his hands. Then suddenly I had a reaction of weakness. What had happened? God spoke to me and told me to ask for what I would like. I got down on my knees and said, 'Lord give me strength, knowledge, and wisdom to do what you want me to do.'

For two days I remained in an intensity of passive surrender. Then the desire to study, something I had never had before, motivated me into action. I rang my minister and asked him to sort me out some suitable books. He arrived armed with huge volumes of theology, interpretations of different Gospels, Confessions of Faith and many others. When I started to read I astounded myself, for not only could I understand them but I was drinking in every word as if I had been thirsty for years. God had given me another of his precious gifts - to be able to discern spiritual truths in the Bible, the Word of God.

The week after my baptism, all sorts of temptations arose. I was offered appointments to social positions, which previously I would have given anything to obtain. One Friday night I was faced with another decision. My minister had asked me to take a Sunday service at church. I knew that this was something which normally a new Christian would have loved to do, but I was so full of natural egotism and pride that I knew I wasn't ready. I would have been glorifying myself if I'd agreed.

On Saturday I was in my kitchen, doing the washing, thinking about it again. Then I made up my mind. 'No I'm not going to do it - not my glory but God's glory. Everything is to be done for the glory of God.'

I had no sooner expressed these thoughts, when I heard the sound of roaring wind in the trees and looked up to see where it was coming from. A light seemed to shine on and through me, giving me an impression that filled my whole being. The roaring seemed to turn to cheers and I felt as if I had given the right answer to some terrific question. I was overflowing with love and joy, a joy so wonderful that mere words cannot express it. This was something I couldn't explain at the time, but I know now that it was God pouring the Holy Spirit on me.

That afternoon I was conscious of the words of Jesus,

'Let the dead bury their dead, but you, come follow me.' Mark 8:22.

'Who me? I'm too weak to follow, I would run at the first thing you asked me to do. What about the persecution? What about the cross I would have to carry? I can't follow.'

Then the story of Peter denying Jesus came to mind and I thought, 'If Peter, who knew Jesus and loved him when he was here on earth, denied him in the critical hour, what chance would I have?' But a comforting thought accompanied it; Jesus forgave Peter because he knows the weakness of human flesh.

I said, 'Yes, Lord, I will follow and I know that you won't ask me to do anything that you won't give me the strength to accomplish.' So I followed, trusting in his strength to be sufficient.

God commanded me to go and teach people to find him. 'Who me? What could I teach them? The only things that I know are all worldly.'

His words came into my mind,

'I will teach you and I will cause you to remember those things which I teach you. Don't worry or be afraid when you are asked to witness. What you are given in that hour that will you say.' Luke 12:12.

On Sunday I was still very happy and the peace and calm was wonderful. Later on that same evening, I found myself thinking up sermons. The thoughts poured out and I was persuaded to take up a pencil and paper. I fought this for some time because I hated writing letters. I'd always avoided anything in this line. After a while, I knew I would get no rest until I did something about it, so I took up my pencil and paper and sat for a moment.

When I started to write, the very first words that came on the paper were 'Teach people to find God.' The next words were, 'A desire to want God above everything else. *Thou shalt love the Lord thy God with all thy heart*; total submission of the heart. *Thou shalt love the Lord thy God with all thy mind*; total obedience to his will. *Thou shalt love the Lord thy God with all thy strength*; total loyalty. *And thou shalt love thy neighbour as thyself.'*

Then came a surging desire to speak to my neighbours and friends, in fact the whole world, about the truths, enlightenments and work of the Holy Spirit. I realised that I was going through this experience for a reason.

On Monday morning at five o'clock I found myself wide-awake with the desire to write again. I started to write stories; the first was entitled 'The Practical Housewife's Approach to Religion'. It was light, breezy and humorous, but with a definite message. At seven o'clock when I stopped writing I thought I'd read what I had written, and it was then that I became conscious of the power of God working through me.

On Tuesday I went to golf as usual and was having a very nice round, but as I approached the twelfth fairway I became aware that I had to write a book. The idea seemed like fantasy, so I paid no more attention. But try as I might I couldn't get the thought out of my head.

On Wednesday morning when I woke up the idea was still there, only stronger. I found myself thinking, 'How can I do such a thing? I just wouldn't know how to start. Why me, when there are others specially trained for this work? What would I do with it if I wrote it?' Assurance came that I would be shown. So on Wednesday afternoon, thoroughly exhausted, I said, 'Lord if it's your will, I'll do it.'

Immediately the voice said, 'Peace,' and my heart was calm once again.

I was afraid to talk about my experiences with John or anyone else. John was a good man, a good husband and father, but he was committed to pursuing his ambitions. My new perspective on life didn't fit with his ideals. The night of my baptism he stayed at work late so he didn't have to come to the service. People didn't talk about the Holy Spirit like he was real in those days. I felt as though my experience was radical and very traumatic.

A week later I visited my minister because I felt I needed to get this sorted out. I discussed the whole experience with him and he wisely told me to be patient, that everything would be revealed in God's time.

Life for the next few days went on as usual, one daughter in bed with measles and the other with mumps, but I was still very conscious of the nearness of God. Several weeks later my minister asked me if I would take the church service in early February and share my experience. I couldn't answer then as I felt I needed time to think and pray about it.

On Saturday night John and I decided to go to the cinema. We chose a musical, 'Teacher's Pet', starring Doris Day and Clark Gable. The plot was about an ace newspaperman being invited to a university to show the students the finer points on story writing. I sat on the edge of the seat and took in everything. He said that to be a good writer you have to take your subject and give it to your readers from all angles - the how, when, where, why and who. You must give the story life.

My story had life - the life we are all seeking so earnestly - eternal life, and accuracy founded in the book of truths - the Holy Bible. I had my cue to start writing.

After a few days I knew I had a message that I had to share, but I didn't know how to start. Nevertheless, I decided to take my pencil and ask God to lead me. The purpose was clear, 'To the Glory of God'. Radiance overpowered me and the words seemed to fly onto the paper without any effort. As soon as the inspiration stopped I would put down my pencil and wait, sometimes for two or three days.

By now there was no doubt in my mind that God wanted me to teach people to find him and to write to his honour and his glory.

The experience of my conversion, which I have spoken about here, was God's unique way of touching me. Conversion is a personal matter - a person's own encounter with God. The way he has dealt with me may not be the way he deals with you, but we can be sure that we will have an encounter if we seek him.

I had learnt how to gain entry into God's kingdom, to be under his guidance, and was discovering his directions. As I look back now, I can see clearly what God has done and the steps that he showed me.

'Without faith it is impossible to please God, because anyone who comes to him must believe that he exists and that he rewards those who earnestly seek him.' Hebrews 11:6.

In Peter's inspired sermon on the day of Pentecost, he shouted,

'Repent and be baptised, every one of you, in the name of Jesus Christ for the forgiveness of your sins. And you will receive the gift of the Holy Spirit.' Acts 2:38.

What did this really mean to me as an individual? I had become aware of God and acted on faith, asking for his forgiveness and cleansing. I surrendered my heart, will, mind and body to God as a sacrifice to him. I was prepared, by the help of his Holy Spirit, to leave the old life behind, and to accept Jesus Christ as my personal Saviour, my High Priest (who speaks to God on my behalf), my coming King, my Lord, and Ruler. I was prepared to obey him then, as now, and through all eternity.

The moment I surrendered to these conditions, I received the presence of his Holy Spirit. There was no mystery, no secret, but just total surrender, acting on faith.

3

Max and the Riptide

For the Christmas holidays our family went to our beach house at Piha, a surf beach on Auckland's west coast. It was only a few days before I received my first assignment from God. I was invited to have a cup of tea with my friend Gay. While we were catching up with the year's events, I happened to say that I hadn't done any of the things that I had proposed for the year as I'd had a personal experience of God.

'Oh,' she said, 'you're just the kind of person my husband Max would like to meet. Would you come tomorrow night and tell us about it?' I said that I would if he was interested. She assured me that they were both very interested.

The next night I went to their home and was greeted warmly. Immediately Max told me that he had been a Bible student for thirty years, that he had an extensive knowledge of the Bible, but that it wasn't sufficient for him.

So I told him about my experience of Christ's sufficiency. We talked about the difference between law and grace. Law demands but grace bestows. Law commands, but gives no strength to obey. Grace promises and does all we cannot do. Law burdens, casts down and condemns. Grace comforts, it makes us strong and glad. Law appeals to self to do its utmost, but grace points to Christ, who takes care of everything. Law calls for effort and strain, and urges us to a goal we never can reach, but grace works God's purpose in us.

When I had finished he said, 'What a wonderful experience, what a wonderful testimony for God. I wish I could know something like that - to be alive and full of joy like you.' I told him that he could, that it is for anyone who will put their hand in the hand of God.

Max said that he was waiting for something, and that when he received it he would be able to give out. 'That's just where you're wrong. God gave his only Son for your redemption, salvation, justification and sanctification. How much more do you want? How about starting to give yourself to God right now? Take what Christ has done for you and rest in him,' I said.

It was as though I had dashed a cup of cold water on his face and he said, 'You've certainly given me something to think about. All these years I've been waiting for something that's already been done for me.'

A week later I met Max as he was about to go for a swim with John. At Piha there is a dangerous rip either side of the bay that has tragically claimed many lives. When you swim there you must keep in the centre of the beach, which is marked with flags and patrolled by life guards, to stay out of danger. A few unusually strong swimmers, swimming outside these flags, have been known to turn the rip to their advantage - they have been caught and carried out beyond the breaker line where the rip dissipates so they can swim towards the centre of the beach. They wait for the huge breakers and body-surf back in.

Max's experiences with the Piha rip had a profound effect on his life. Later he wrote about this and what happened to him the day he went swimming with John. Let Max tell the story:

> *'Chumps! That's what they are, complete and utter chumps! I'd no more swim in that raging, dashing turmoil than fly. What pleasure can there be in taking a route like that when there's the whole of the beach to swim in?'*
>
> *If I have said it once, I must have said it a dozen times, as I have stood*

on the elevated Tasman look-out, or other such vantage point on Piha Beach, and watched in amazement the antics of the swimmers in the swirl of the out-going rip. What a sight! Turmoil, pounding waves, dangerous rocks, swirling waters and people all mixed up together - almost enough to make the uninitiated observer signal for help. That is how it looks from the distance - almost as though there was no hope for those poor unfortunates of ever getting out alive.

'Quick, the binoculars please! There's someone I know. Yes, it's John. Thought he would know better than to go in there.' People in trouble always cause concern, but as I watched, little did I realise, that some day, at John's invitation, I too would swim in that same turmoil in his company, as equally relaxed and unconcerned about the turbulence, as a close look through the binoculars showed him to be. Little did John realise, as he relaxed in the swirling rip, that looking down on him from that vantage point was a man who was about to learn from just such an excursion, a most practical lesson in what it means to abide by faith.

There are some things in life, deeply spiritual, which can be illustrated by many and varied day to day experiences. Likewise, the day by day experiences, if approached in faith, will always lead to the 'calm beyond'.

The day arrived. I was sitting on the beach watching the crowd enjoying themselves in the surf. Many times I had swum out beyond the breakers, but had found it always an exhausting experience. You are never sure that you will get there before being forced to turn back through sheer force of circumstances. A surf swimmer quickly learns to appreciate the inner voice that says, 'It's time to turn back.' For once the energy of the physical is exhausted, the swimmer is entirely at the mercy of the sea.

One day, lured by the thrill of it all, and confident I could swim half way to Australia, I swam out, and out, and out. The going was good, so were the breakers, but they were behind me now, and under the spell of some impish instinct to keep going, I did just that. Then realising that I had to turn back some time, I looked toward the shore. Big men looked like pygmies, and children looked like ants; the sea in which I had been revelling, suddenly lost its attraction. Solid ground was a long way off! Distance didn't lend enchantment to the scene.

With determined strokes I headed for the shore, but it was a long way even to the breaker line. I was all alone. The easy strokes of the outward swim were no longer easy, and under the exertion of anxious endeavour, even my best effort didn't seem to bring me nearer the shore. I reached the breaker line, but to my alarm, I had so exhausted myself in the long swim that I was unable to mount the breakers, which normally would have carried me swiftly in a body-surf toward the shore.

It then became a struggle for survival. No sooner had one breaker passed over me, than another pounded in on top. 'Swim for it,' I said to myself. But the waves I had swum out through so confidently, now made me feel very humble in their merciless pounding.

All the confidence had gone. It now seemed there wasn't even time to breathe, and I needed all my energy to keep afloat. All I needed to have done was to raise my arm, and I would have had all the resources of a very efficient surf club at my disposal, but in spite of my rapidly weakening condition, I would not raise my arm - for no other reason than sheer pride.

I was well aware of my need, but decided not to submit myself to the humility of being brought ashore, until the very last. Maybe, then, I would be too late! How I longed for the feel of solid sand under my feet. Many times I tried to touch bottom, but it only seemed to make matters worse. When at last I did touch with the tip of my toes I had almost decided to signal for help, but with renewed hope, I tiptoed until I was able to stagger out of the water.

Still with a sense of pride, and not wishing to be seen in an exhausted condition, I lay on the sand just out of reach of the water. I don't know how long I stayed there, but I had never known the sand to feel better. The thoughts which went through my mind contributed firmly to my new found good reason to believe that man, at his best in any capacity, is very puny.

For a long time I wouldn't swim out of my depth after that. Indeed, I don't think I ever did until John saw me on the beach this day and said, 'I'm going round the rip. Would you like to come with me?'

What a difference it makes to be able to approach the problems of life, even those with an element of risk, in the company of a friend. When the friend is big, and strong, trustworthy and has been over the road before, it takes away the fear and concern you otherwise would have if going it alone. What is more, to know that your friend could and would support you in difficulty is sufficient to encourage you to accept his invitation.

Such was John. I had seen him in action many times, and knew him as a friend. Without a second's hesitation, and in spite of the scare of my long swim alone, I knew I could trust him.

It is easy to review the past and acknowledge the leading of God in so many ways - he, who loved men, even while yet sinners, to such an extent that he sent his Son Jesus Christ, that he may not only be their friend, but that in a very real and competent way, their all in all - yes even life itself.

Whenever the opportunity allowed, Joyce spoke to my wife and me, concerning spiritual things. Life with God, and the mediator between God and man, Christ Jesus, had reached a stage where even pride could not subdue the God-given instinct producing in us a conscious need of help. Stimulated by the radiant evidence of Joyce's calm, assured approach to the adequacy of life in Christ Jesus, we were submissive to the working of the Holy Spirit in our own lives.

Tired of the fruitless effort of 'try, try, try again', and confused in mind by the screeds of religious jargon which in so many cases serves only to frustrate the grace of God, we humbly bowed to seek God's forgiveness for the past, and plead for the leading of his Holy Spirit in the future.

Undoubtedly, the Holy Spirit was already formulating the 'Riptide Story' in Joyce's mind, even as we passed her on the beach. With a twinkle in her eye like the beam of a lighthouse beacon, she said, 'Go on Max, you won't drown.'

The current carried John and me safely past dangerous rocks, through the pounding waves, to the calm beyond. To me it was a most exhilarating experience. As I floated past the Tasman lookout and looked up at some people who were looking down on us, it occurred to me that those who simply stand off and look can be completely wrong in their judgment. As we were steadily carried out and out, the thrill of accomplishment, going places, getting there, and completely without physical assistance, so filled me with the joy of life that I felt like calling out, 'Come on into the waters.'

After half an hour, Max came back to me with a smiling face, thrilled that he had been caught in the rip and survived. He said, 'I've been wanting to do this for two years and at last I've plucked up enough courage. I'll never be afraid of the rip again.'

I awoke suddenly at two o'clock in the morning, and wrote the 'Riptide Story':

On the shore at Piha one man was telling another about his risky plan. He was saying, 'You know, there's no need to go out through all those waves to get to the calm outside the breaker line. If you'll come with me I'll show you how to ride the riptide to the calm beyond. Instead of being exhausted, and too tired to enjoy surfing back, you'll be fresh and ready to tackle the waves.'

Nervously the other man consented, so they stepped into the water. They had only gone a few yards when they felt the pull of the rip. The novice was told to relax and not fight it. He knew before he took that step into the water that he couldn't turn back - the riptide is so strong that once you are in, you must ride it to the finish.

Out they drifted past Partakei Rock, the novice thinking that he could well be dashed to pieces; on they swam past the treacherous Camel Rock, out again past Beehive Rock and finally finished up at the back of the breaker line. Here they just lay in the calm water, the swell peacefully rocking them to and fro.

They waited. A big wave came and they rode it safely back to the beach. What a thrill! The novice was overjoyed at the apparent ease with which he had attained something that he had been striving to do for years. At last he could ride the sea with confidence!

I've ridden a riptide - not the one I've just told you about, but the riptide to God and eternal life. One day I had the invitation from God to ride the riptide with him and I, like the swimmers, was terribly tired of being with the crowd in the froth and bubble. I struck out by myself, but the going was too tough, I was caught in the froth and bubble of life and at times it threatened to overpower me.

Then I called on my Lord and Saviour to show me the way to the peace and calm beyond. I heard his voice gently persuading me to take the first step.

After a lot of thought I nervously put my foot into the sea - groping a bit at first. Then I felt the strong hand of God take mine and there I was, being kept safe in the riptide. Out I went past the rock of repentance, past the rock of Baptism, past the rock of total subjection to God, to the calm and peace of God's everlasting arms. After God had refreshed me with his gifts, he said, 'Go ride the sea of life with confidence, teach people to find God - guide them to eternal life.'

Are you still standing on the beach today, the same as you were last year and the year before, busying yourself with the froth and bubble? Are you being dragged helplessly, struggling with the rip? Let me take you by the hand and show you the way to be kept safe by Jesus Christ our Lord. Call on him and follow him, and you will find yourself not drowned but rather pulled towards God our heavenly Father and eternal life.

The next morning I gave Max the story. The following week I saw him coming down the road to my house. I could see straight away that he was different. His first words to me were, 'Joyce, I've given myself to Christ.' He recounted that as he had received the story, the Holy Spirit had assured him, saying, 'This is the way, walk in it.'

Those of you who have seen the birth of a little baby will agree that there is nothing more wonderful. Wonder, amazement and joy are mingled together. But have you seen a man reborn? The joy is unspeakable.

4

Tested and Following On

The holidays were over and it was February. I had written my personal testimony and now I knew that I had to accept the invitation to take the church service. Naturally I was nervous about the thought of standing in the pulpit as God's servant, knowing my own inadequacy, but I couldn't turn back. My minister was conducting a Bible Class camp and he had left the entire church service for me to conduct.

As the organ was playing I stood in the vestry and prayed for Christ to be my strength in my hour of weakness. As I walked down the aisle and into the pulpit all my nervousness vanished, and as I spoke my voice rang out loud and clear.

In the front row I saw Max and Gay and their four children. Max explained afterwards that he and Gay had made the long journey to be present because, just as God had used me to help them in their riptide, they now felt that their presence and prayers could help me in mine.

I can't remember all I said, but from different people in the congregation that morning, I learnt that some were deeply moved and grateful that I had spoken about my experience. By special request I was asked to repeat the service in the evening a month later.

At last the day arrived. As my minister and I were making the final arrangements, he asked me if I would be prepared to make a 'call' at the end of the service, asking people to accept Christ as their saviour. This presented a problem. I wasn't sure what I should do. My minister said that it was entirely up to me to do as I felt. When I asked some of the people at church what they thought, one said, 'Maybe they'll think that you think you're Billy Graham' (the great American evangelist).

I answered, 'We haven't got anything against Billy Graham have we?'

Another said, 'Maybe the people won't like it, with you just being one of them.'

Finally I said, 'Leave it to me. I'll go home and pray about it, and let you know this afternoon.' At home I prayed, 'Lord what would you have me do?'

His answer came immediately. I knew with certainty that I must make a call. Clearly I was faced with a challenge. I thought about the possibility of someone wanting to accept Christ and that if I, through fear of ridicule, failed to give the invitation, that person may be lost for all time. I knew that I had to make a call and I was prepared to make a fool of myself for Christ.

As the service drew to a close, I extended an invitation for anyone who wanted to make a decision for Christ or to rededicate themselves to him to come to the front of the church

As the organ began playing the final hymn, a young woman stepped from the back of the church and came forward. When I looked down at her my heart opened and God's love poured from heaven through me towards her. After this service some of the congregation and my friends, who had come specially to hear me, came home to supper along with this young woman. How happy she was. She had given herself to the Lord. She told me that she'd come over twenty miles to hear the service. How happy I was. God had not let me down. He had not let me be ashamed.

John also came to hear me. I did so want him to see what God can do when a person allows God to work through them. The next night I said to him, 'Well, what do you think about it?'

He replied, 'I've never seen you so confident. How could you speak with such boldness?'

The only way I could explain it was, 'As I walked up the aisle into the pulpit my heart filled with the love of God, and that cold, icy hand that grips your heart when you stand on the first tee of the golf course, when you're playing the championship tournament, just didn't get a chance to take hold of me.'

For the next six months life was wonderful. I had found joy, peace and a future that mere words could not explain. As I went about my daily chores attending to my family and their needs, I kept saying to myself, 'All this and heaven, too.' But this was only the beginning.

I was now attending church regularly on Sunday and my children were attending Sunday School. At last this was the life I wanted. But there was something missing. I looked around and for the first time I was fully aware that John was not with me. It never occurred to me that I would have to go on my own. We had always done things together and I thought he would always be beside me.

Suddenly I was overcome with a sense of loneliness and I wanted to turn back for him. I found myself going back down the path until something blocked my way. In my mind's eye I saw Jesus. 'You wouldn't crucify me again would you?' he asked. I took one look at his lovely face, turned, and took off up that path as fast as I could go, never to turn round and look back again!

As the weeks went by, I sought to walk along God's way and John continued along his own track. Two people cannot live together and go separate ways and be happy. Yes, we could put up with each other, but the fellowship, the sharing of mutual interests, and the joy of talking things over was no longer there.

At first I was rebellious towards God. I didn't think it was right. Then my rebellion focused on John and I couldn't understand why he didn't want Christ to completely control his life. I prayed and prayed, and asked God to change his heart and spiritual perception.

Feverishly I started to scheme and work out how I could get John more interested. I tried to entice him to church by taking him to film evenings. I tried inviting people home who might say the right word at the right time. The harder I tried the worse things seemed to be. John resisted fiercely and was always on guard, defending his ideals. He knew that I was pushing him. He was no man's fool.

At last, thoroughly beaten, I went back to God. 'Lord I've tried. I can't win him. I can't bring him into the kingdom. Only you can. I'm going to put him in your hands, Lord, for you to work in and through him your will.' The beginning of God's victory was the admitting of my defeat, my inability to do anything by myself. I entered a deeper peace with God, content to leave everything in his hands.

We women are great organisers, and we're often guilty of organising other people's lives - of trying to force God's hand to suit our particular ideas.

By this time the seed of new life was flourishing within me and its growth couldn't be denied, but the travail for that life to express itself was very painful. Women know that the birth of a baby can only be accomplished by the person who has conceived. So it is with spiritual rebirth. I was the one who had chosen this life. It was me and only me that God was going to deal with. Conversion is only the conception of the new life. From here on God was leading me into the abundant life which Christ has the power to give. He says,

'I have come that they may have life, and have it to the full.'
John 10:10.

I busied myself with God's work. I became a Bible Class leader and a speaker at ladies' meetings. My desire for knowledge was very keen, so I took a Bible correspondence course for eighteen months with the N.Z. Bible Training Institute (now Bible College of New Zealand). When I completed my first examination paper, I was hesitant to send it in, imagining it would come back with a red pen through it, marking it 'rubbish'. Bible Study was so utterly new to me. I had no confidence at all. But, when the results came back and I opened the packet very nervously, there on a little piece of blue paper was written '79%, an excellent paper'. I just couldn't believe my eyes. That result inspired me to complete the course.

5

The High Price of Love

As a new Christian, I was full of what God had done for me and what he was willing to do for every one else if they would let him. Some people said to me, 'What kind of a God is he who divides a husband and wife? He calls one and the other doesn't come.' These words often rang in my ears and challenged me.

I came to realise that when we are called by God, we must come out of 'the world'. We must take our priorities away from the possessions, distractions and influences that divert our attention and keep us from focusing on God. We must give up the world in our hearts. The words of Jesus spoke deeply to me.

'Do not love the world or anything in the world. If anyone loves the world, the love of the Father is not in him.' 1 John 2:15.

My world was first and foremost my husband, children and home. It isn't strange that this was where my Christian battle commenced. Jesus says,

'Do not suppose that I have come to bring peace to the earth. I did not come to bring peace, but a sword. For I have come to turn a man against his father, a daughter against her mother, a daughter-in-law against her mother-in-law - a man's enemies will be *the members of his own household. Anyone who loves his father or mother more than me is not worthy of me; anyone who loves his son or daughter more than me is not worthy of me; and anyone who does not take his cross and follow me is not worthy of me. Whoever finds his life will lose it, and whoever loses his life for my sake will find it.'* Matthew 10:34-39.

'For it has been granted to you on behalf of Christ not only to believe on him, but also to suffer for him.' Philippians 1:29.

I gradually discovered that Christians have not been given an easy road and those of us who have taken Christ as our personal saviour have also enlisted for the Christian fight; we have a battle on our hands. But look what Jesus our leader says,

'I have told you these things, so that in me you may have peace. In this world you will have trouble. But take heart! I have overcome the world.' John 16:33.

As a comparison, let's look at God's dealing with Abraham (then called 'Abram') in the book of Genesis in the Bible.

Abraham lived with his father and two brothers and each one of the sons took a wife. The whole family shifted into the land of Haran and through to Canaan. The family was prosperous and wealthy - multi-millionaires by today's standards.

It all began for Abraham when the Lord said to him,

'Leave your country, your people and your father's household and go to the land I will show you. I will make you into a great nation and I will bless you; I will make your name great, and

you will be a blessing. I will bless those who bless you, and who-
ever curses you I will curse; and all peoples on earth will be
blessed through you.' So Abram left, as the Lord had told him;
and Lot went with him. Abram was seventy-five years old when
he set out from Haran.' Genesis 12:1-4.

Let's look at the passage from a real life point of view. Abraham hears
the Lord tell him to get out of the country, away from all his relatives
and to leave his father's house. Abraham probably lived with his father
and family for forty-five years and in that time he would have worked
hard, tilling the ground and making rich pastures. He would have taken
great pride in planting trees, erecting buildings to house his family and
servants, and he would have been greatly attached to his life in Haran.

Can you imagine what kind of home Sarah must have had with servants to keep it spic and span, its beautiful hand-woven drapes, its hand-
beaten silver and gold plates and vases, her fabulous jewels which she
took great pride in displaying at social functions? And now the Lord
told them to leave it all behind.

Some time later God tested Abraham when he asked him to give up
his son.

God's instructions to Abraham were,

'Take your son, your only son, Isaac, whom you love, and go to
the region of Moriah. Sacrifice him there as a burnt offering on
one of the mountains I will tell you about.' Genesis 22:1,2.

The passage goes on to tell us that Abraham rose early in the morning,
took Isaac and went to the appointed place. But can you imagine what
the previous night must have been like for Abraham and Sarah?

If they discussed the plans, Sarah would have said again and again,

'Are you sure Abraham? You must be mistaken. Isaac is God's gift to you and if we sacrifice him, where will this 'great nation' originate from? God's promised us that. Why not give God Ishmael?' Ishmael was Abraham's son by Sarah's handmaid Hagar, born because Sarah had been unable to conceive.

But God didn't ask for Ishmael, he asked for Abraham's special son - the person he loved most in all the world. Can you imagine Abraham, loving Isaac above everything else, the child of his old age, turning to Sarah and saying, 'The Lord's will be done. I can't understand this, but I'm going to obey'?

It took three days to journey to the place God told him to go. Isaac started to wonder what it was all about. Eventually he said to his father, 'The fire and wood are here, but where is the lamb for the burnt offering?'

And Abraham, still trusting God, replied, 'God will provide himself a lamb.'

After they had arrived at the place of sacrifice, Abraham bound Isaac and placed him on the altar. He raised the knife to plunge it into his son and suddenly the Angel of the Lord called out, 'Abraham! Abraham! Do not lay a hand on the boy. Do not do anything to him. Now I know that you fear God, because you have not withheld from me your son, your only son.'

Caught in a nearby thicket was a ram - God had provided a sacrifice in the place of Isaac because Abraham was obedient.

These two events happened way back in the 'dim dark ages', as people say, but let's take a look at things from a contemporary point of view.

When we grow to womanhood, we start thinking of our future - a husband, love, children, a home where we can have freedom of thought and action. Then eventually we get our man. But, instead of thinking of

The High Price of Love

him as just a man, we begin to build him up in our hearts as something really out of this world, we put him on a pedestal and worship him.

Then we get our own home, it's much nicer than Mrs. So and So's. We start to build this up in our hearts until it's not just a house we live in, it's a palace! Now we have created our own altar and our own god. After we have served these, we may perhaps have time to go to church once in a while, to keep up appearances.

It was the realisation that I needed something greater in my life than all this that started my search for God. True to his word, when I knocked, he opened and received me to himself. I surrendered my will to him so that he would be Lord in my life, and decided to serve only him. Here was a new person coming to take charge. Little did I know at the time that it was I who had to dethrone the old reigning monarch and smash the altar.

Events happened that eventually led to the change of my mindset and gave me new values.

John came home one night with a request that hit me like a bomb and shook me to the very foundations. He wanted me to mortgage my home, my security, so he could buy a launch. A boat was the last thing I wanted. I hated the sea and couldn't even look at a boat jogging on its mooring without being seasick. I couldn't see any future in this. John's face was radiant with the thought of ownership. I started to put up all the arguments in the world, and in return he put forward all the wonderful advantages as he saw them. But I wouldn't yield. He was asking for my security. John could have taken the money out of the business, but this would have reduced the buying power. My home, which I now felt was threatened, had ceased to be just a building to live in. It had become my security, and nothing could change my mind. I could only see John's request as jeopardising our security. I didn't want a mortgage around my neck. It would endanger my freedom. I wanted to be free from all encumbrances.

That night I took my problem to the Lord and asked for his guidance. His answer was, 'Sacrifice and love are the price.'

But the other voice kept chipping in, 'You're mad if you do what he wants. Your security will be gone. You've worked all your life for this. You're not going to let him take it away are you?'

A few days later, John was on the phone and said, 'I have to decide today, the offer closes this afternoon. It's up to you Mum, it's your decision.' Everything seemed to be in a whirl. My head kept saying, 'It's unreasonable; it's your security,' but the love in my heart for John overruled all.

The still small voice kept encouraging me saying, 'Sacrifice and love are the price.' I agreed, admitting that I must be doing the right thing for it was certainly given out of love and sacrifice.

For a few days I went about feeling like Samson must have felt without his hair. With my security gone I found myself more in prayer with God, saying, 'Why does this have to happen to me?' Christians are supposed to be happy and I felt ghastly. 'Why does it have to be me?'

Then I heard that still small voice say, 'I will be your security.' God as my security. It had never occurred to me that God wants to be our security as well as the life that is in us. I rushed to be close to him and as I nestled closer into his presence, I knew that I would be secure for all time. My heart started to rejoice, and I thanked God for this experience and for teaching me the folly of trusting in material things.

The summer season was approaching, and the next big crisis arrived. John wanted us to go away every weekend in the boat. But I had my Bible Class to teach in the morning and I regularly attended church. The children went to Sunday School. I knew that I was facing another major decision.

In seconds the whole of my life before I became a Christian seemed to come before me; all the wonderful times we had had together; the joys we had shared and the anxious times of sorrow when we had consoled each other. We had been happy because we were alike. We had shared in common a desire for the things of the world.

The decision was mine. In a voice that didn't even sound like mine, I said, 'I cannot give God up for you. God comes first in my life.' I had to reject the weekend's pleasure cruising and chose to attend church with my children.

I've learnt a lot from these experiences and there are lessons that I'd like to pass on.

It isn't God's will to come between people. He is always searching for the lost. His servants are always calling people to repentance. If you're not in the kingdom of God the fault is yours. Unconfessed sin is like an iron curtain between God and man.

'This is good, and pleases God our Saviour, who wants all men to be saved and to come to a knowledge of the truth.' 1 Timothy 2:3,4.

It is God's will that you accept Jesus Christ as your Saviour and enter the kingdom of Heaven. What is your will? Do you want to? The decision is up to you.

A Christian becomes mindful of spiritual things. The moment a person accepts Christ as Saviour, they realise the necessity of keeping God's commandments, obeying his will and living in the new regenerated life. On the other hand Satan, as prince of this material world, has devised some wonderful imitations. He seeks to keep us busy with all sorts of pleasures. He offers us the chance to worship cars, houses, boats, sport - purely for a person's own glory, pride, selfishness and alcohol to promote a sense of wellbeing.

I came to understand that sin always causes heartache, and that we women can be terribly wrong. We have no right to expect from any home or husband what only God can give us. It is when we put all things in their proper place in our lives that we can have peace with God. We must give up the worldly love that is demanding and possessive, and exchange it for God's love that is giving and forgiving.

The Old Testament story of Abraham is my story today. Is God asking you to give up your old way of life and begin a new life where he will lead you? Is he asking you to sacrifice the 'Isaacs' in your life? 'Ishmaels' won't do - you must sacrifice what you love most so that God can reign as King in your heart. Do it today, take everything and offer it on the altar of sacrifice and love.

My life's ambition is in the Holy Trinity - God who is love, and whose love passes all understanding; my freedom in Jesus the Son, who purchased my freedom with his blood on the cross; and the Holy Spirit my security, it is through his teaching, his knowledge and his wisdom that he makes known the truth - God's love towards us and the accomplishments of Jesus for us. It is in God's promises that we can rest, secure and confident in Christ's victory.

'But take heart!' he says, 'I have overcome the world.' John 16:33.

6

The Recipe for Success

You often hear people say, when you start to discuss Christ with them, that they find no need to go to church and have fellowship with other Christians. They say that they can be just as good sitting at home or doing the things that they want to do on Sunday. What harm can be done walking around the golf course on a lovely Sunday morning, or building their house, or pulling the car to pieces, if this is what they want to do? They're happy doing that, surely there's no harm in it?

There's an old song that goes, 'I'm a lonely little petunia in an onion patch.' When I first heard that song I really felt for that petunia! Little did I know that in the years to come I would see a wonderful lesson in that song. Would you grow a petunia in an onion patch? Of course not, the onion smell would overpower the sweet smell. If I saw a petunia coming up in an onion patch I would soon transplant it to the flower garden. What warm comfort would a little petunia get from an onion, except to cry and bemoan its fate day after day?

God has given us his church so that Christians can come together in fellowship and worship, and although we must go out into the world to work, we know that on the Lord's day we can be refreshed for the coming week, we can be still and know that the Lord is God.

If you really want to be a Christian mix with them, worship with them and the sweet fragrance of God's presence will soon permeate your whole being.

Is your life wonderful, thrilling, exciting, and full of adventure? Perhaps you think if only you could go on a world trip things would be better. Or perhaps it's a new car you need. Maybe the house is shabby and needs doing up. Perhaps you're tired of your husband and you feel sure that if you could get a new one, life would be wonderful.

But these things won't really make any difference. In a few weeks they too will become old and shabby, and you will be discontented again. It's not new things you want, but a new self - the opportunity to leave behind mistakes and regrets and to start a brand new life guided by Jesus Christ.

Jesus says that you must be 'born again' if you would enter his kingdom of peace.

The man to whom Jesus spoke these words in the first instance was Nicodemus, a leader in the Jewish religion. He was a good man and kept the Ten Commandments to the letter. Jesus told him that this wasn't enough, that he must be born again (John 3:3).

Nicodemus was very interested and said, 'Lord how can this be? It's not possible for me to enter my mother's womb again.'

Newness of life is given by God's Spirit who dwells within us the moment we surrender our hearts and wills to him.

I would like to tell you a story about a woman who was planning a dinner party. A recipe for a lovely dessert had been given to her sometime previously, so she thought she'd make this for her guests. However, when the time came to make it, the recipe was missing. 'Never mind,' she said. 'I'll do it my way.' But the result was a mess and a failure. So she rang up her friend and asked for help.

On arrival, the friend took one look at the mess and said, 'You can't do anything with this,' and emptied it into the kitchen bin. With recipe book in hand, she said, 'We'll start again,' and before long the dessert was ready and perfect.

Perhaps we've forgotten God's recipe for life. Perhaps we can't be bothered to look it up, and so we've gone ahead like this woman and made a mess of everything. But don't go to your neighbour with your problems, go to Jesus, who says,

'I am the way, the truth, and the life. No man comes to the Father except by me. Behold I make all things new.' John 14:6.

Have you ever thought of a new self? A new life with all the old mistakes and failures cancelled out? To enter into this wonderful life, we must seek Jesus and ask him to guide us, which he will do by his Spirit.

You have a problem. You would like to seek Jesus, but you just can't give up the old life.

We have a wonderful promise to take care of this.

'Yet to all who received him (Jesus Christ), *to those who be-lieved in his name, he gave the right to become children of God'.* John 1:12.

When my daughter was nine, she decided that she would like to grow some vegetables. She took a packet of carrot seeds and sowed them. Some time later I went out and saw two beautiful lines of lovely green carrot tops. I knew I had to thin them out, so I proceeded to do so.

As I was doing this, people's words kept coming to me, 'I wish I could live a life like you keep telling us about; I'd love to come to Christ, but I have so many other things that take up all my time. Perhaps later on when I'm old and can't do the things I do now, I will come...'

If the carrots aren't thinned at an early stage, the whole crop will be stunted for lack of food and room to grow. The time comes when room and food will make no difference to the growth of the baby carrot, and it eventually shrivels up and dies. This is true of spiritual life too. We need to make space for God's work.

My life used to be crammed with golf, skiing, and social engagements - so busy that there wasn't time for anything else. But when the seed of Christ fell into the middle of it all, it was then I started to weed, to allow the seed to flourish.

Christ grows in the centre of my life and casts a shadow on the glamorous, the bright and shining things of this world, so that they lose their appeal. It is Christ who is the light and life of a Christian.

7

In God's School

As people heard about this change in my life, I was invited to give my testimony at meetings in and around Titirangi. I was happy to do this as it was close to home, but one day a lady asked if I would speak at the Y.M.C.A. ladies' meeting in Auckland city.

I told her that I'd have to think about it. Going into town was getting a bit out of my depth. The old voice started to speak, 'You don't know who might hear you and where you'll be asked to speak after that. No, don't go! Get out while the going's good.'

I had just about decided not to go, when this verse came into my mind,

'No one who puts his hand to the plow and looks back is fit for service in the kingdom of God.' Luke 9:62.

That was all I needed, so I went. That day I met a great Christian lady who asked me if I would be prepared to speak on rebirth at a meeting that she was conducting.

God had told me to write, to take up my pen, and I found that he had enabled me in this. When I was asked to speak at ladies' meetings, I would pray and ask God for a message, because I had no message of my own, and he would inspire me with a message which I would write down.

This was the first time I had spoken on a particular subject and I stuck so rigidly to what I had written that I almost read my address word for word. At the end of the meeting another Christian lady came up to me and said, 'That was a very good message you gave this morning, but do you mind if I give you a little advice?'

I said, 'No, say anything that will help me to do the work of the Lord better.'

She said, 'Don't keep so rigidly to your notes - just let the words flow, let the Holy Spirit speak through you.'

I said, 'I couldn't do that. God has told me to write and I speak the message that he has given me. I'm afraid that I might speak some of my own words.'

'You're limiting God,' she replied.

'Oh no,' I said, 'I'm not ready to do that kind of thing yet - I've only just begun this work. Maybe in three or four years I'll be able to, but I must grow slowly.'

She put her hand on my arm and looked me straight in the eyes, and said, 'There isn't time, grow like a mushroom, grow like a mushroom. One day you may be asked to speak impromptu and then you wouldn't have time to write your message down.'

When I got home, I thought about what she had said. She was right; I trusted God because I could see the words on the paper, but I wasn't prepared to trust him to put the words in my mouth. It was only a matter of days before I was put to the test.

This lady, of whom I've been speaking, was asked to address a group in Titirangi, and I volunteered to drive her there. The meeting wasn't at my church, nor was it anything to do with me. She gave a wonderful address including an account of part of her own personal experience. God had blessed her considerably.

At suppertime the President of the ladies' group walked out of the kitchen and apologised for the unavoidable delay with the tea. She looked at me very sweetly and said, 'We have Mrs. Mitchell with us tonight. Would you be good enough to say a few words?'

I nearly died! I swallowed hard and said, hoping she would give me a lead, 'What would you like me to speak on?'

'Oh, just whatever you feel led to say.' I looked over at my friend, but she had her head down and wouldn't look in my direction. I searched my brain but there wasn't even a word there, let alone a message, and I knew God was my only hope.

The story of Moses flashed before me, how God had called Moses to lead the Children of Israel out of bondage to the Egyptians, and to trust him for the right words. When Moses asked God to send someone else, God was angry with him, because he needed to trust God in order to be given the ability.

I knew from this lesson that if I didn't get up there and then I would never be able to speak. As I stood up I prayed, 'Lord, I'm going to get up - I'm going to open my mouth and I'm relying on you to fill it.' The words came and I experienced in a new way the wonder of trusting the Lord and of taking him at his word!

For months I had been going around with a gag in my mouth, but that night it was taken away and I was free to speak God's words. I gave thanks to God for his goodness and saw acres and acres of green fields, in which to work, before me. I knew that I had been called to be a spokesperson for God.

God was using me to win souls for his kingdom and my enthusiasm was rising greatly; seventeen of the nineteen girls who were in my Bible Class made the decision to give their lives to Christ.

Again I was compelled to write, but I couldn't see that people would want to read anything that I produced, so I conceived an idea of my own. Instead, I decided to start another Bible Class and invite young married mothers, to teach them to find God. I was putting great preparation into this plan. Then one night, as I was reading my Bible, God spoke to me through an episode in John's Gospel.

Peter was required to wait for the Lord's command, but he got tired of waiting.

'I'm going out to fish,' Simon Peter told them, and they said, 'We'll go with you.' So they went out and got into the boat, but that night they caught nothing. Early in the morning, Jesus stood on the shore, but the disciples didn't realise that it was Jesus. He called out to them, 'Friends, haven't you caught any fish?' 'No,' they answered.
He said, 'Throw your net on the right side of the boat and you will find some.' When they did, they were unable to haul the net in because of the large number of fish. John 21:3-6.

I was going to work for God in the way I wanted, but I was going against God's plan for me. That night I knew that I must cancel my plans and carry on with God's plan, no matter what I thought of it.

As women we must be careful that we don't lead ourselves astray. God's ways are not our ways. Don't be a religious butterfly flitting from this church to that or from this doctrine to that. Find out by prayer whether you're carrying out God's plan for your life. Let me illustrate this with a story about a wealthy woman.

The lady of the house was about to go out, so she called her housekeeper and issued instructions for the day. The only job that she wanted done was to have the carpet vacuumed. Then off she went. Now the housekeeper was a keen worker and, looking around the house, she saw that the blinds and windows needed cleaning, there was washing to hang out and there were several other odd jobs to be done, so she busily threw herself into these tasks.

The lady of the house arrived home and the housekeeper came to report. She had cleaned the blinds, cleaned the windows, hung out the washing, and done several odd jobs. But the lady of the house said, 'That's fine, what about the vacuuming?'

'Oh!' said the housekeeper, 'I was so busy doing the things I thought you'd like done, I didn't have time to do the vacuuming.'

Unless we carry out God's command and do his will, we are no good in the kingdom of God; with that in mind, I started to write.

8

'Learn of Me'

If only someone had told me at the beginning of my Christian life to learn from God.

Have material things ceased to interest you? Have you got a knowledge deep down inside that there is a great deal more to life than what you've been able to find? Perhaps some of us are despairing, but instead we should be rejoicing because we are on the brink of the greatest discovery made possible to humankind. It is when we come to the end of ourselves that we come to the beginning of God.

> 'Come to me, all you who are weary and burdened, and I will give you rest. Take my yoke upon you and learn from me, for I am gentle and humble in heart, and you will find rest for your souls. For my yoke is easy and my burden is light.' Matthew 11:28-30.

We picture the word 'yoke' as a wooden frame across the neck and shoulders of two oxen to which a very heavy burden is attached with chains. We picture the drover, with his whip and coarse language, urging these unfortunate animals to perform their nigh impossible task.

The word 'yoke' also has another meaning and this is the meaning that Christ meant, for in my life I've proved it to be so. It means to 'unite', 'pair', and 'link to one another'. Christ will ask us to work with him, not with a heavy yoke on our shoulders, but by his Spirit, which lives within us. We will walk, but the word and the responsibility are his.

After I'd accepted Christ and was standing at the foot of the cross, Jesus said, 'Follow me,' and then seemed to disappear. I wanted to follow but I didn't know how. I had a long list of requests for God that I would pray every day. I went to a friend and asked him if there was something else I should do.

'Only if you're not satisfied with God!' he said and offered no more advice.

Of course I wasn't satisfied with God. How could I be? I'd only just met him. I wanted to know him better, to love him more, and to serve him.

It was like going to your father when you're in a boat and saying, 'Dad, I'd like to learn to swim.'

If Dad was of the old school, brought up the tough way, he'd pick you up, throw you overboard and say, 'Swim. That's the way I learnt.'

Well, that might be all right for some. But there are others who need gentler handling. Unless we're told, we might flounder around for years, keeping up so we won't drown, but never making any progress.

I went away from this friend, from whom I'd sought council and received such a blunt reply, sad and lonely. But it's in those times that you hear a word of encouragement. A voice kept saying, 'Learn of me, learn of me.' (Matthew 11:29). So I started to learn of Christ - who he is, why he died, why he rose and what he is doing for me in his glory at his Father's right hand. I learnt of his nature, of how his Spirit is born in me and how, if I present my body to him as a living sacrifice, he will work his blessed plan in and through me.

I learnt through love and faith to bare my heart, and to let God remove with his pruning knife the things that held me in bondage and were killing my very soul. I learnt to love him in a way that demanded my life, my all, just as his love for me demanded his life, his all, on the cross for me.

To learn of him is like feeling the warm sun on your body after being covered all winter. Your soul stretches up, putting out more roots to take a firmer grasp of the everlasting life that flows from his glorified body. All the things that I had been asking God for were already mine. This is the kingdom of God.

I was deeply hurt by my friend, but as the weeks and months went by, training in Christ's school, I could see why I'd had to pass through this experience. One day I phoned my friend and told him that I had been hurt, but now I wanted to thank him for his rough treatment. I had gone to lean on him but he'd thrown me straight back into the arms of Jesus. His boat had been full and he knew that it was time that I should learn about Christ for myself.

How many of us in the church are content to stay in the minister's already overflowing boat, content to let him pull us to safety? We should be prepared to take the oars and go out seeking on the sea of life for souls in danger of drowning.

If we would only cease from pleasing ourselves for three months and learn of Christ, and what he really is to us, we would all enter more deeply into God's peace.

What is God's peace like? It isn't like after you've had a children's party, and the last little guest has gone home, and your own are tucked up safely in bed. You pull up a chair to the fire and sink into it, kick off your shoes which have been killing you for the last half hour, and with a huge sigh, say, 'Peace at last.' Tomorrow, as soon as day breaks, there will be something else.

God's peace is a peace deep down - a confidence in God's ability to sustain you no matter what. Only the born again Christian knows it because it's the Spirit of Christ living in you.

As I look back over my experience in God's school, not once was I eager to serve him. There was always a battle of wills, the realisation of my human weakness, my inability to perform the tasks. I was resentful of having to give up my time and made the excuse that there were others specially trained for the particular task. In the beginning, we tend to look on service as a chore or nuisance inflicted on us. It is only when the will has been surrendered that the victory is won and the ability given.

What made me submit my will to God in all these instances?

Service became a challenge to my faith in salvation through Jesus Christ. Surely the same Christ, who I trusted implicitly to save me from my sin, could also enable me for service.

We believe in the sufficiency of Christ. We know that he has done all that is necessary for us to have eternal life, but it's so easy to let Christ's sufficiency make us lax or unwilling to serve him.

Service requires a faith that leans on God's grace to supply the strength, knowledge, wisdom and ability to perform that which he asks us to do. In acknowledging our weakness to him, he is made strong in us.

Just as the sufficiency of Christ has saved you, it will also enable you for service. If our faith is not sufficient for service, is it really the faith that enables Christ to save us? It is by grace through faith that we are saved. The question we should constantly ask ourselves is, 'I am satisfied with Christ, but is Christ satisfied with me?'

Service isn't a chore or an inflicted nuisance, but the expression of the light and life of Jesus Christ who now dwells within us.

'In the same way, faith by itself, if it is not accompanied by action, is dead.' James 2:17.

Some women I meet say that they can't serve God in any great way, but at least they can make a cup of tea or wash the dishes for someone. This is highly commendable, but we women must rethink our faith. We limit God because we bring him down to our level instead of letting him draw us up to his. Christ says, 'I will draw all men up because I am lifted up.' (John 12:32). Why don't we let him do that?

We have got to learn to think big with God. God is a creative God. An almighty God. A sovereign God. The God we serve and worship is the God who spoke and the earth came into being. He is a big God. It's he who is going to do the work. Don't limit him by your small ideas of yourself. This is not inflated ego, but allowing God to glorify himself through us. How much more time do you and I need to go on proving that, by ourselves, we can't do anything?

In Matthew 19:26 Jesus says, 'With me all things are possible.' He also promises us that we will be able to do greater things than he did when he was here on earth, because he has gone to his Father. Are we allowing him to do these greater things through us, or are we just making a cup of tea? We have to dedicate everything we do to him and allow him to take us further.

We must come to a place in our lives where we let God do our thinking. We must learn to think big because God's resources are unlimited.

9

Boats on the Sea

John's boat was the last thing I wanted, but the final decision had been mine. Now the house was mortgaged and John had his dream boat, *Triton*. It was forty-five feet long, fast and powerful with twin engines - the envy of the boating community. John bought himself a captain's hat and one each in different colours for his crew, Gail, Christine and me. He was a happy man.

Our first summer boating holiday was one I'll never forget. Our cruise was to be to Kawau, Rakino, Waiheke and Ponui Islands in the Hauraki Gulf for three weeks.

On Christmas Eve, with all supplies ready, we went down to Westhaven where our boat was moored. A strong north-easterly was blowing straight in and the sea was very choppy.

After experiencing great difficulty in holding the dinghy still, we managed to load a few supplies, and John took the oars. We couldn't put too much in because the waves kept splashing over the sides. We had to travel a few hundred metres to where *Triton* was moored. It looked for a while as if we'd never make it. The wind and tide were slowly taking us away from the boat. Encouraging John with the words that he'd have to row harder, we finally made it. I boarded *Triton* with the supplies while John returned for the children and the remaining gear.

I went to work putting fresh meat, butter and milk in the refrigerator and all the other jobs that have to be done before going on a cruise.

Still on the mooring, the boat was jogging and bucking and I had great difficulty keeping my balance. Eventually everyone was aboard and John was very relieved.

Then it happened. 'I must get off,' I said. 'I have to get off.'

'Why, what's the matter?' asked John, very concerned.

'I'm seasick,' I cried. We had to leave the boat and go through the performance of getting back to the wharf.

Driving home on Christmas Eve and having to stop on the road to be sick was no picnic. All I could think of was that people would assume I'd had too much festive cheer.

The wind hadn't dropped at all in the night, but in the morning we went down again to the boat to see what it was like. White faced people and unshaven men were chattering like monkeys. They'd boarded their boats the night before and decided to ride the wind out on the moorings, but the wind hadn't obliged and most of the families were seasick.

Now that I was well again, John wasn't going to let this weather stop him. Those with smaller boats were amazed that John would tackle the sea. All supplies were on and all we had to do was weigh anchor and go.

I took my place at the wheel with the two engines running smoothly, and slowly nosed the boat up to the moorings so that John could let them go. The wind was so strong that it took all his strength to stand. I had the two children on the flying bridge with me and John was busy tying the anchor into place.

We came out of the breakwater into quite a big sea, and as we turned westwards the north-easterly hit us broadside on. The boat rocked, tins crashed, bottles clinked, saucepans fell and children screamed - I didn't have time to worry. All I knew was that I had to get the boat around. It was up to me! Leaning all my weight on the wheel, round it came and we had the sea running behind us. It took five days for the wind to blow itself out, but we tucked away in a sheltered spot to weather the storm.

I'd never been cruising on a small boat before and I didn't know that everything has to be stowed before sailing, regardless of weather conditions. I learnt from boating that you always have to be ready and prepared so that whatever conditions you meet, you'll be able to tackle them.

After three weeks at sea with refrigerator problems that arose a few days into the trip, I was very glad to get home and put my feet on solid ground. For the next two days, as I stood in the kitchen doing the dishes, the dishwater had a peculiar way of coming up to meet me as the effects of the motion of the sea on my equilibrium slowly wore off.

By now I'd learnt to take all my problems to the Lord in prayer. Seasickness was a problem that I couldn't overcome and I tried everything. At last, thoroughly beaten, I asked God to help me.

Our next summer cruise was only three weeks away and the thought was a nightmare. I kept praying and believing that God would help. While I was buying stores and getting the linen aboard I kept telling him that I believed he would do something. It was the night before the cruise and I said, 'Lord, I still believe that you'll do something for me.'

A small voice within me seemed to say, 'I'll take away your seasickness, but the boat must stay.'

I thanked him for his answer and yielded to him more. From that moment I have never been seasick again or felt the motion of a boat. John was amazed, so I had to tell him what had happened. The boat took on a new interest for me. It had become part of my life for a reason and I wanted to find out why people loved boating so much.

As with most things, the *Triton* lost its glamour and John wanted to have a boat built to his own specifications. As the plans were drawn up he had the lines of a Fairmile in mind. The boat was to be fifty feet long and constructed of the best materials. Over the eighteen months that it took to complete building, he went to view progress every week.

John asked me to officiate on launching day. I broke a bottle of champagne on the bow, naming it *Trinidad* after the destroyer that John had served on. The chocks were removed and the boat slid slowly into the sea with the cheers of the spectators.

We had a celebration lunch and while I was busy serving sandwiches and tea, John came in ringing wet. He had a startled look on his face and said, 'I fell in.'

I couldn't stop laughing and he wasn't very happy, but he saw the funny side later.

I learnt to handle the boat and experienced the thrill of mastering the helm. There is a wonderful peace on the water and God spoke to me often while cruising. I wrote a number of stories about the lessons God taught me through those experiences.

I'd talk to people and they'd say how wonderful boating was; to be able to pack up on a Friday night, leave all your worries behind and enjoy yourself in the peace, exploring new bays and islands. Then, when a storm is blowing, to tuck up in a nice, quiet, peaceful bay behind the cliffs while the wind and the storm go roaring over the top. There were dozens of little things that I could now understand. I could see boating from their point of view.

One day I said to John, 'Now I know why people love boating. I've been with you and worked alongside you and experienced it for myself.'

Boating is to some people what God is to me. I find my peace in God, my shelter from the storms of life and my exploring in his Holy Word. Worries are left behind at the wharf, but you can be sure that they're the first thing to greet you when you return home. God says, 'Come to me with all your worries and I will give you permanent rest.'

The Trinidad

People may be able to shelter from a storm, but what about life's storms? They may be able to get away from other people, but where can they go to get away from themselves?

I learnt that before we pass judgment, we have to give a fair trial. I gave boating a fair trial for four years, but I wonder how many people would be prepared to give God a fair trial in their lives before they condemn him?

Putting yourself under one who knows makes the subject so much easier to understand and helps you gain confidence. Ignorance breeds fear and you can't possibly enjoy anything of which you're afraid.

Perhaps you've tried to be a Christian but failed so terribly that you're afraid to start again. You have to bring yourself under the training of the expert Jesus Christ, who will teach you and show you how to enjoy the abundant life found in him.

Although I knew that God had called me to service, there were times when I tried to reason why. I couldn't see that I had any particular qualifications for his work. How could he use a woman like me?

These questions were answered one day as we were cruising on the Waitemata Harbour.

We were rounding North Head, when a sturdy little tugboat steamed past us in a terrific hurry. In the entrance of the Harbour was a huge liner, moving slowly and cautiously. The tugboat looked tiny and insignificant as it drew alongside and fastened itself with ropes.

On our launch John said, 'That little tug's going to bring that huge vessel into the wharf.'

We watched the tugboat bring the liner up the channel past dangerous rocks and shallows and eventually, with much pulling and swirling water, the liner came to rest at port.

I said to John, 'How can such a little vessel manoeuvre such a huge liner?' He told me that tugboats have no surplus fittings, only those that are necessary to generate power.

As well as having the tugboat to pull the ship into port safely, there is also a pilot on board the large vessel. The pilot is an expert in navigating the harbour.

The ship is precious to its owners and they want to be sure that no mishap befalls it. Another thing that occurred to me is that while it's on the high seas, there is no need for a pilot or a tug, all the danger is close to the destination.

How true this is of people on the sea of life. They are milling around the entrance to the peace and rest that is offered in Jesus Christ, but only a few allow themselves to be piloted through. Some get caught in the shallows of procrastination while others are wrecked on the rocks of pride.

We are God's tugs and pilots which he sends out on the sea of life. Although we are few in number, we go out with the power of the Spirit of God. I realised that day that I didn't need any qualifications of my own. God was able to supply the power I needed in my life to serve him.

If God is calling you, don't be afraid - trust him to give you the power to do what he asks you to do.

10

On Course

When we sailed down the Harbour, I would cast my eyes around and see a boat here and a buoy there. Further on, rocks would be ahead and each time as I was looking at these things I would steer towards them. John said to me one day, 'Have a look at the course you're steering, look back at the wake.' I was terribly surprised; I had no idea that I was so far off course. He said to me, 'You need to take a bead or a point on the land ahead and keep your eyes on it and make sure you line the bow up with it.'

Now that's perfectly logical when steering a course and I thought how true it is for steering our heavenly course. We must keep our eyes on Jesus and heaven, and line ourselves up with him.

Our third season of boating was now approaching and I was really looking forward to our cruise.

By now we had got used to the boat and knew what it was capable of. It wasn't surprising that John suggested going to the Bay of Islands in Northland, but to me the journey seemed quite out of our range. The children were only seven and eight and I felt that John should have another man on board to help him. A forty-five foot launch is quite a handful for one man and a woman on the high seas. But he told me that I was as good as a man for a crew and that we could do it easily.

Naturally I was nervous because I knew the kind of seas that are encountered around Cape Brett.

John said, 'Let's chart a course together and see what you think about it then.' He took a map and dividers and started to plan the sixteen hour trip.

The first part of the journey was to be to Kawau Island, which is three and a half hours from Auckland, where we would wait for favourable weather conditions. The next leg would be Whangarei Heads, which is another four hours from Kawau, and then still further North to Whangaruru, and finally Russell. The rocks and reefs were well marked on the map and I had confidence in John as a sailor and a navigator. With a course mapped out the planned trip seemed quite straight forward, and having a mental picture of what we were doing and where we were going made everything very simple.

I was quite willing to go and as soon as conditions were right, we sailed. The weather was beautiful and everything went according to plan until we reached Whangaruru. This was a lovely harbour and we decided to spend a few days there. But unfortunately the weather changed and northerly gales kept us there for a week. It was a good place to be caught because the anchorage was firm and we could moor within a few yards of the beach. We were as snug as could be.

We made two attempts to get out, but each time we were driven back. After a week we decided to make a dash for it. The waves were huge but John and I agreed that if we didn't try to get through we might never get to Russell. The children were tucked up on the lower berths so that if they fell out they wouldn't hurt themselves. Our hearts were set on the course and off we went.

We were going up one wave and down the other, but somehow we had no fear, only determination to get through. I stood by John's side ready to take over the wheel when he was tired. I was on the wheel as we rounded Pearcy Island, just off Cape Brett. Owing to the roughness of the sea we had to keep well out so as not to get caught in the backwash from the land. We had the sea behind us and I found it hard work holding the boat on its course as we surfed down the waves.

Deep Water Cove was just around the corner so we made for this haven to have a rest and breakfast before going on to Russell. How wonderful it was to be in a place such as this after being pounded by rough seas. As John and I talked over our achievement, I could see so clearly another side to this experience.

I said to him one day, 'You know John, how simple a journey like this is, if you take the time to study the map and to use a compass. When a family knows its objective and has a planned course, with their hearts set on the one destination, each can lend a hand and pull their own weight with harmony and co-operation.'

Today in the world there are millions of families who are going no-where. They have no map, no compass and no destination.

11

Stepping Stones

'To each is given a bag of tools,
A shapeless mass and a book of rules,
And each must make, ere life is flown,
A stumbling block or a stepping stone.' - The Webb Institute.

Obstacles, trials and tribulations are part of the Christian life. Jesus says,

'In this world you will have trouble. But take heart! I have over-come the world.' John 16:33.

How are we approaching these tribulations and what are we doing with those obstacles? Do we baulk, afraid to take them on? Do we pray to God to remove them or, like the trained athlete, do we take it all in our stride?

There have been times in my life when I've sat down and said, 'Why does this have to happen to me?'

I was at home by myself one Saturday night, studying the Scriptures and sitting an examination paper for a short story writing course, when all of a sudden I stopped. 'Why am I here when I could be out having a jolly good time?' I asked myself. 'What good am I doing? What use will it all be? Perhaps I am just wasting my time.' Questions and doubts pressed into my mind.

That night God spoke to me through the story of Joseph, the favourite son of Jacob (Genesis 37-47). Joseph's dreams showed that God had his hand on him but it was necessary for God to discipline and train him for the work ahead.

His own brothers cast Joseph out from the family, from luxury to poverty, from an easy, joyous life to slavery, from a life full of people he loved to loneliness. He was purchased as a slave by Potiphar, an officer of Pharaoh and captain of the Guard.

But Joseph didn't sit down and cry to the Lord, 'Why does this have to happen to me?' No! He went about his work, forgetting himself, and concentrating on how to please his master. This pleased the Lord and he blessed Potiphar's house for Joseph's sake.

Through many experiences the Lord never failed Joseph, who eventually became Governor of Egypt with control of huge storehouses of food in a time of great famine. Then Joseph's ten brothers, who had made their way down from Canaan, stood before Joseph to buy food, unable to recognise him.

Here was a chance for Joseph to get even but, when he asked them to bring their other brother, they had to admit that they were guilty of selling Joseph as a slave.

Seeing their repentance, Joseph wept. They were tears not of self, but of compassion, for the sight of his brothers had touched his heart. Through his faithfulness Joseph made each one of his trials a stepping stone, until at last he was in a position to feed his hungry family.

One of our biggest stumbling blocks is rebellion - refusing to be disciplined. Perhaps we have suffered unjustly at another's hand, but do we hold a grudge against that person or do we take it as a discipline from God? Joseph could have refused his brothers food, but instead, he wept and satisfied their hunger.

I prayed to God that night to make me like Joseph, always ready to feed my family with the 'Bread of Life', to teach and live God's Word, and never to count the cost.

Joseph became a great influence for good in the lives of many people, and you and I have the same opportunity today. Women and mothers have great influence in family life. I don't suggest they 'wear the pants', but Mum is always on hand, and children tend to lean more on her and confide in her their problems and fears.

It's then that we can prove ourselves to be stepping stones or stumbling blocks. We are often asked questions about nature, about God and Jesus, and children have no problem believing that God exists. But what is your attitude towards God and Jesus? Is he something abstract, or does he really live in your heart? If you don't really know God, how can you possibly introduce your children to him? If you neglect your duty to God, to make him Lord of your life, to know him personally, you are the first stumbling block in your child's spiritual life.

Are you preparing your children for life or are they being only half prepared? A person consists of body, mind and spirit.

'Yes,' you say, 'I've always studied their diet - plenty of vitamins, enough sleep, plenty of exercise; they could run a five minute mile! I've given them the best education the country can offer, although I've had to go back to work to keep them at university.'

What about their souls, their spiritual lives? Let's be blunt. Do they know Christ? 'No,' you reply, 'I've left that part for them to decide. When they've made their way in the world they will have time for that.'

What would have happened if you had allowed them to choose their own diet from the time they were born? Or if you hadn't shown them and taken their hands when they were learning to stand and walk? Obviously, they would have had little chance of survival. Is that what you've done with their souls?

We are constantly reminded about food through advertising media -

vitamin A for this, vitamin B for that. But don't let us get so concerned about the vitamins for the body that we overlook the 'Bread of Life'.

How is your son or your daughter going to react when facing their first temptation - the first stormy weather on the sea of life? Will their character snap because you fell down on your job? How cruel and inconsiderate can we be to our children?

You would say, 'How ungrateful,' if your child pointed a finger at you and said, 'It's your fault Mum - you sent me out not fully equipped.' Don't fall down on that part of the lives of your children. Make sure they are equipped with the Word of God, that they have Jesus Christ to pilot them over life's stormy seas.

I was having a cup of tea with a fifteen-year-old boy, and the conversation turned to spiritual things. He said to me, 'I have a cup and saucer in my hand. How do I know it's a cup and saucer? Because my mother told me when I was little. Why don't our parents tell us about God the same way?'

The time will come when our children will lay the blame at our feet. It's our responsibility - yours and mine - to teach our children about Jesus. As they grow up and have greater understanding, Christ will present himself to them in a very real way, and they will know him. They won't have to learn who he is, they will have been taught by you, their mother. God himself will then take over to make them fit for his service.

How do we become teachers to our children and families? A good teacher is one who allows herself to be taught first. Spend time each day in prayer and Bible reading. At first you may find it an effort, but once you fit it into your routine, you'll find that you look forward to it.

Are we allowing God to teach us by life itself, or do we rebel, feel sorry for ourselves and sulk? We should make each experience not a stumbling block, but a stepping stone to a more fulfilling life with Christ.

12

Youth's Challenge

Youth is a wonderful time in a person's life - young in heart, full of energy and adventure, ambitions and dreams. It's also an important time because life-changing decisions have to be made.

Over the past years the behaviour of some youths has not only shocked us but has also left a sick feeling in our hearts. To many it has brought despair. What's happening to our youth and what's the remedy?

I'd like to take you back to when Christ walked the streets of this earth. What were the youth like in his day? We have the example of the prodigal son who rebelled against his father's authority and walked out to squander his money and substance in wild living.

A woman was brought before Jesus to be judged because she was caught in the act of adultery. A rich young ruler came to Jesus and asked how he might enter the kingdom of God. When he was told he had to sacrifice his wealth, he turned away sad because Christ was asking too much.

Are not these the same problems that youth face today? Has the world changed so much during the last 2000 years? Perhaps the fashions, the tempo of life, the way of living have, but the hearts and desires of youth are still the same.

Some say, 'Whip 'em, bring back the cat-o'-nine tails and they'll soon come to heel. Lock 'em up for a couple of years until they cool down and that'll fix them.' That certainly isn't the answer - it only makes them sullen and more bitter than ever.

What is causing this upheaval in youth? If there's an effect there's always a cause. The cause is our nature - we find it much easier to do evil than do good. Where does our nature originate from? We inherit it. From our parents to their parents, we trace it right up the family tree, until we arrive at the first parents, Adam and Eve. The original sin committed by these, our first parents, continues to curse humans down through the years, and will continue to do so until this world is destroyed.

You say, 'If that's so, what hope have we for our youth?' There is not only a hope, but there's also an established fact: we can exchange our old 'Adam nature' for a brand new one. Jesus makes this dynamic statement,

> *'I tell you the truth, no one can see the kingdom of God unless he is born again.'* John 3:3.

How do we get born again? It's a physical impossibility, but Jesus is referring to the 'inner person' - that person we know so well. Do you want to exchange your inner self?

Who do we exchange our inner self with then? Jesus says,

> *'You diligently study the Scriptures because you think that by them you possess eternal life. These are the Scriptures that testify about me, yet you refuse to come to me to have life.'* John 5:39,40.

There you have your answer. New life comes from Jesus. As parents we have a great responsibility. We see the dreadful curse hovering over the heads of the youth and yet we hear some say complacently, 'Oh well, it's the times; it's the world we live in.' With the first threat of disease, we have our children vaccinated. But this other infection, that can destroy their souls - we just sit back and say, 'What's the remedy?'

The greatest gift and remedy we can give is the truth of Christ. He loves these young people and died for them; only he can transform them. He places inestimable worth on their lives and calls them to great things.

But in this world, the task of presenting this truth is never easy. To be successful at the job you are about to undertake, you must first desire perfection. Without desire there is no will. You must generate enough enthusiasm to do something about it, and then finally trust, have faith, and act accordingly.

When we are young, we worship our heroes. You know what I mean; a girl, about thirteen, gets a crush generally directed at some pop singer. 'He's my ideal man, he's amazing!' Sure he is, if that's the kind of man you are looking for.

To the youth I would say, if you want a real man, a redeemer, saviour, and friend, turn your eyes to Jesus. Get a vision of Christ and make him your hero.

We dream, we are ambitious, but let's be sure that we get our values right before we proceed too far. Remember all that glitters isn't gold. Nor does a wonderful picture contain everything.

I want to tell you about something that happened in my life that was one of the best lessons I've learned.

One night when I was twenty and on my tropical cruise and the moon was just right, two other girls, three lads and I, decided to experience a postcard dream for ourselves. We asked the stewards to prepare us a picnic basket and rugs. On shore we hailed a taxi and went to a beautiful beach called Moonlight Bay.

It was wonderful, just like the picture; white sands, blue water, green palms and a lovely moon. We spread out the rugs and opened the picnic basket ready for the fulfilment of our dream. But the picture hadn't told the full story - it had only shown us the wonderful things, the enticing things. As we sat down to eat, something happened.

To our horror, within seconds we were covered with huge black sand flies and could they bite! We had the picnic packed, the rugs up and were back in that taxi before you could say 'Jack Robinson!' We finished up having our picnic on the deck of the *Monowai*!

Beware of things that look wonderful on the surface, or appear to be harmless. Go a little deeper to see if there are any stings before you do them.

There are hundreds of young people walking the Christian life very slowly. Some are just letting the seed of new life lie dormant. They love Christ, but they've never become aware of what Jesus really means to them.

He says, 'I will be your strength; I will be your patience; I will be your courage; I will teach you all things, I will cause you to remember everything I have taught you; I will tell you what to say.' He promises to go before us in any task he asks us to do.

If I were to give any of these young people a souped-up BMW, do you suppose they would take it home and lock it in the garage, and just keep telling themselves that they were the owners of a fast car? No, at the first opportunity they would have it out on the highway with their foot on the accelerator as hard as they possibly dared. It is only then that they would really know the thrill of ownership.

Why don't we take the restraints off our spiritual lives and become aware of the ability available through Jesus Christ our leader?

The challenge goes out to the youth today. What do you think of Jesus? Repent and take by faith what Christ has done for you on the cross. He has paid the price for you but you have to claim, choose and accept that new life for yourself.

13

Winning Our Families

After I had spoken to a ladies' fellowship meeting on one occasion, a member of the group rang and asked me for help. A number of their members were Christians, but their families weren't. These women wanted to know how they could win their families for Christ. This became a burden to me. I was in the same position. What could I do? I asked the Lord for a message and two verses came to mind that set me on fire.

'If we ask anything according to his will, he hears us. And if we know that he hears us - whatever we ask - we know that we have what we asked of him.' 1 John 5:14,15.

Then I read this verse:

'This is good, and pleases God our Saviour, who wants all men to be saved and to come to a knowledge of the truth.' 1 Timothy 2:3,4.

Our families can be brought into the kingdom of God by prayer. As I was praying about what to say to the group I saw, as it were, a stream of women entering through the clouds into heaven. It was as if the Lord was saying to me, 'Win the wife and you can win the whole family.' The Lord was calling, but it seemed incredible that he was asking me.

This verse loomed up before me:

'He could not do any miracles there, except lay his hands on a few sick people and heal them. And he was amazed at their lack of faith.' Mark 6:5,6.

In the light of that, all I could do was pray, 'Lord, I believe you can do this work through me, help my unbelief.'

As I prayed for the right way to deal with the problem, he spoke to me through another verse:

'First take the plank out of your eye, and then you will see clearly to remove the speck from another's eye.' Luke 6:42.

When I asked him to help me do this, I entered a new relationship with Christ which meant that I was now his responsibility. It was up to him to hold, keep, guide and enable me, and I found a new freedom from self-effort. In this new relationship it no longer mattered to me whether my message was received with enthusiasm or not.

The removal of the beam out of my eye was not pleasant. I wanted desperately for my family to know Christ. One night when I tried to persuade them, one of them said, 'Let me see the change in your life and then maybe I'll consider it.'

Those words rang out like a challenge, and I yielded to God still further.

The people we seek to win to Christ are worldly. If we are unattractive, selfish, quarrelling and despondent, and if their 'worldly goods' and pleasures offer them a better life than that which they see in us, why would they want what we have?

I asked God to search my heart and reveal what was wrong in my life. There were dozens of things: pride, impatience, intolerance, selfishness and many others too numerous to mention.

'Lord,' I prayed, 'I cannot overcome these things, but you can.'

God also taught me about love, that there are two kinds. There is the kind we lavish on people because they fulfil our desires. We love them for the joy, comfort and protection they give us. This was the kind of love that I had, selfish and receiving.

So I prayed, 'Lord, show me your love,' and John 3:16 came before me.

'For God so loved ... he GAVE.'

We need to compare ourselves to 1 Corinthians 13. If our gifts and work aren't motivated by love, they are selfish. Our love is selfish if we love for what we'll get out of loving.

The spiritual love of a reborn Christian is a giving love. There is only one way to obtain the love that Paul speaks of, and that is to yield more to God. Unless the evidence of God is in us - love, joy, peace, patience, kindness, goodness, faithfulness, gentleness and self-control (Galatians 5:22-23) - God is not in us. Let us yield to his perfect love, so that God can radiate through us and out to our families, and to all those we come in contact with.

A woman's job is a full-time one and it's important not only for the physical, but also for the spiritual wellbeing of our families. Christianity isn't just a Sunday affair, but a life to be lived every day. We are home-makers and with this goes the responsibility of setting a moral and physical standard. If our standards are low, we cannot expect high standards from our children.

The church is where we go to have corporate worship and fellowship, to hear and learn what the Word of God says to us as individuals. Our minds assimilate the message and it goes deep into our hearts.

Our homes are the places where we should practise what we've learnt. It's no use sitting in church every Sunday unless we put that learning into practice and become better people, able to live a better life.

To bring Christ into the home is no easy matter. It's only natural that as we're all of different temperaments, each of us will see life from a different angle. We each have individual problems. Our forms of recreation are different. I've realised over the years that we can't please everybody and, as wives and mothers, we certainly can't please ourselves.

When I became a Christian, I faced that fact and decided that I would please God first. By taking him into my heart I took him home to dwell with me, to be my strength, my love and my all. Life is less complicated when we aim to please just one person.

To be successful in business or any undertaking, to succeed in life, we need a plan. We have to have an aim. What is your plan for the future? What is my plan for the future? I'm aiming high, to the very top - the kingdom of God. On what foundation have I laid this plan? On Christ himself who says,

'I am the way and the truth and the life. No one comes to the Father except through me.' John 14:6.

There were two brothers discussing the question of marriage. One had found a lovely girl. She came from the right side of the street; her parents were successful in business and her future seemed to be promising. However, one brother was a committed Christian and he said, 'Yes, you know where she's come from, but the vital question is, do you know where she's going?'

Modern marriage is built on a home with labour saving devices, cars, luxury and pleasure - material things. As they wear out, so does the foundation, and lives built only on this fold up.

God has a plan for each of our lives and if you prefer to stay out, then on that great day, don't blame him for leaving you behind.

There's a definite place for us in the church and it's part of our privilege to extend the church into our homes. The important question is, 'Is there a place for Christ in your heart, in your home?'

Be sure that Christ has his way in your life first, before trying to put other people's lives right. Wherever Christ is, the social order of things will be better, not because of the people but because Christ is working in the hearts of those people. Readiness to do the Father's will is the true test of a Christian life. To hear Christ's words and do them is to build on a rock that will endure. To hear and not do, is to build on shifting sand.

The woman's place in the church is right alongside her minister, working with him as he teaches and shows the truth in Christ, by seeing that truth is reflected in her life, trusting in God's grace to be sufficient for all her needs. From this day on may it be your plan and mine to take the kingdom of God into our homes and out into the wider world.

14

A Wedding

Once I was invited to a big Chinese wedding held in a Chinese Presbyterian church. We received our invitation printed in gold letters on a red card. Inside was another red card on which we had to reply. The invitation came from the bridegroom's parents and the wedding reception was at their expense.

What a wonderful custom! It reminded me of the wedding we Christians are waiting for with great expectancy. The bridegroom (Jesus) is preparing to take a bride (the church). God his Father has given each of us a special invitation and it's written in the blood of Jesus.

'For God so loved the world (you) *that he gave his one and only Son, that whoever believes in him* (that is, accepts salvation) *shall not perish but have eternal life.'* John 3:16.

The invitation is on a red card, but if we want to attend the wedding we have to accept personally what Christ has accomplished for us. We answer on a red card and our acceptance is recorded in the book referred to in Revelation.

When God prepares the wedding feast and the trumpet sounds to summon us, will you have answered your invitation, or will it still be on the mantelpiece behind the clock? You intend to reply one day, but you won't have a place card unless you answer.

Is procrastination depriving you of your privileges in Christ? Some people are waiting before they take the next step.

Remember Moses leading the Israelites out of Egypt to the Promised Land, and how God protected them with cloud by day and fire by night. When they arrived at the Red Sea they saw the enemy following and began to blame Moses for taking them out of Egypt, only to have them killed in the desert. But Moses said to them, 'Have faith and God will deliver us.' On God's command Moses lifted his staff above the waters. A terrible wind blew and parted the waters, and the Israelites crossed to the other side on dry land. When they had crossed, the water surged together again and the enemy drowned.

Then came the testing period. These people spent forty years in the wilderness being maintained by God on manna and quail. Imagine it, in front of them was the Promised Land, but they were too afraid to go forward and take it. They lacked faith.

In those days we know that women didn't have the same rights and privileges as today. Men held all the authority in that culture. Imagine yourself out in the wilderness getting the meals ready: stewed manna for breakfast, roast quail for dinner, stewed quail with manna sauce, roast manna with quail sauce, quail and manna hash, quail stew with manna dumplings - for forty years! What an existence!

Those of us who have accepted Christ as Saviour are in the same position today. True to his word, God has saved us and is maintaining us. But have we taken the Promised Land by faith? Are we walking with Christ now and obeying his commands and entering into the joy of eternal life? Or are we wandering in the wilderness, eating the same old food every day?

Don't rest on your salvation. Walk with Christ now and through all eternity. You don't have to wait for anybody. God gives each one a special invitation, 'whoever'; that means you. You have to accept it personally. Nobody else can do it for you. You go first in faith and fasten yourself to Christ. Then others will follow.

15

The Tired Christian

During a conversation with a lady I hadn't seen for many years, I told her about my conversion. She was thrilled to hear that after the sort of life I had led, Christ had finally won me. However, she also said, 'I've been a Christian for twenty-five years, but the glow has dimmed. Your glow will go after a while too.'

That remark has been made to me time and time again. When I arrived home I was disturbed by what she had said and prayed to God for a message for the tired Christian.

God said,

'I am God, the same yesterday, today and forever. I am the unchangeable God. Heaven and earth will pass away but my word will never pass away.' Hebrews 13:8.

God doesn't change towards us; it's us who change towards him. We let other things dim our view, clog up the springs from which the living water flows and our Christian lives begin to stagnate, shrivel up and bear no fruit. We have no lustre of our own and any that can be seen is a reflection that depends on how close we are to God.

What is the solution if we have lost the way? There is one solution: to go back to the starting point.

'Come to me, all you who are weary and burdened, and I will give you rest.' Matthew 11:28.

These are the words of Jesus not only for the sinner, but also for the tired Christian.

Cast your mind back and recall the day you accepted Jesus Christ as your saviour. Take a fresh look at him - look carefully. He still has that loving look, he still holds out his pierced hands for us, he still says, 'I am making everything new' and he still wants to live his life in us. This is where most of us go astray. When we accept Christ, we have to let him decide where we're going.

How do we give ourselves to God? The same way we put the rubbish out on Monday morning. Give yourself to Jesus, and he will be responsible for you. It is then that we have freedom in Christ.

The 'flesh' will well up now and again, Jesus has warned us how wicked our hearts are, but he will be responsible. His blood will be applied to the confession we make of our sins. We can stop trying on our own behalf and look to Christ to work in and through us. He has the power to give us a new life.

Why is it necessary to come to Christ? Firstly to appropriate by faith his blood, his death on the cross and his ascension. We go there to present our bodies as a living sacrifice to God. From that minute, we give up all claim to ourselves, put him in charge of our lives and let him tell us where we're going.

If somebody gave you fifty dollars with certain restrictions - ten dollars to be spent this way, ten dollars to go to charity, and whatever is left over for yourself - I know what you would feel like telling that person to do with the fifty dollar note. If we give fifty dollars to a person, we relinquish it and rely on that person's good judgment to spend it profitably and wisely.

We can come to the cross to present ourselves for rebirth, and to give ourselves to God without restrictions. We, as women and mothers, know that birth is a painful thing. But we have to submit to the pain before nature can work. The result is joy in the birth of new life.

We are here to present our souls to the Great Physician so that he can cut out the imperfections. In the kingdom of God there are no anaesthetics. The sore is exposed, the knife does its work and then the soothing healing of Christ is applied. God, the perfect Physician, is quick and sure, according to our willingness to allow him to work.

When God uses the knife on our hearts, cutting away the habits and desires that enslave us, he makes all scars radiant. He uses these scars to deepen our lives, enhance our personalities and to give us greater understanding.

Knowing these things, we are often reluctant. We are afraid of what God might ask us to do. We start to draw away from God and our lives start to lose their glow. We might be asked to travel alone, to go to a foreign mission field, to give up the pleasures we enjoy, or we might be asked to suffer persecution. Do these things hold you back? I knew I couldn't accept any of them, but the love of God was too strong for me and I submitted.

Being human, however, I made one condition - that he wouldn't ask me to do anything that he didn't give me the strength to do. It's on that condition that I follow, and Jesus has never let me down. All that is needed is to follow. His strength is more than sufficient. Won't you try again today in Christ's strength?

I've heard it many times from other women - and I know that it's true of myself - we're perfectly capable of doing a normal day's work, but if we start to worry about something, we just pack up and go to pieces. We lag behind and life becomes a drudgery and burden.

How can we overcome this? Perhaps a friend could come in and take over. That would solve the work, but what about the worrying? I used to be an expert in worrying so I feel qualified to speak on this subject.

When we come to Christ, we come as we are, with all our imperfections, our worries, our troubles and our fears. That's how I came, standing there, burdened with these things. And the Lord says, 'Take up your cross and follow me.'

How was I to take up the cross? My arms were already full and I had no room for anything else. I looked at him, puzzled, and he said, 'Put your burdens down at the foot of the cross.' I did that. 'Now,' he said, 'take up my cross and follow me.'

It's as easy as that. All our worries are taken care of at the cross. Christ will replace your bundle with the cross - to sinners it is foolishness, degrading and shameful so they draw back from it. But to those who believe and carry it, it's the power and wisdom of God; it's no burden.

We come to the cross along the same road as Christ came, with its shame and degradation. On that side of the cross we receive cleansing, but when we take up the cross, we go to the resurrection side, the glorious side, the victorious side.

16

What Prayer Means to Me

I can't recall the number of people who have told me over the years that they aren't able to pray aloud with other people.

When I was first converted I wanted to join with the older Christians in prayer. I went along to the meetings, but somehow I became strangely mute. A prayer would come to me, but it couldn't get past the lump in my throat. Tears would fill my eyes and I knew that if I could speak I would be crying, so naturally I just kept quiet. For weeks I sat in prayer meetings going through this agony.

Eventually I took this problem to God. Instead of telling a friend I told God just how I felt about the whole position.

When I prayed at home in my bedroom, I always prayed in silence. One day I was prompted to pray aloud. It was strange at first hearing my own voice praying. I was crying, the tears falling down my face as I poured out the burdens of my heart to God. After a while I got used to it and experienced greater freedom in prayer. At last the victory was won and I managed to get out a very short prayer at the next meeting.

The purpose of prayer is that God may be glorified in the answer. We cannot glorify God unless first of all his kingdom is established in our hearts.

Prayer is a privilege given to the Christian whereby we can come to God, to wait upon him for his strength, knowledge, wisdom, ability and health which are forever flowing from the Throne of Grace.

A Christian without prayer is like Samson without his hair; like a bird without wings; like a lover without someone to love.

Prayer means that we can speak to God on behalf of our families, friends and neighbours. We can pray for them to enter the kingdom of God. We have an assurance,

'that if we ask anything according to his will, he hears us. And if we know that he hears us - whatever we ask - we know that we have what we asked of him.' 1 John 5:14,15.

We have the assurance that it's God's will for them to come into the kingdom.

'This is good, and pleases God our Saviour, who wants all men to be saved and to come to a knowledge of the truth.' 1 Timothy 2:3,4.

There's a law of prayer that we have to understand. Jesus teaches us,

'If you remain in me and my words remain in you, ask whatever you wish, and it will be given you.' John 15:7.

'I am the vine; you are the branches. If a man remains in me and I in him, he will bear much fruit; apart from me you can do nothing.' John 15:5.

'If you remain in me and my words remain in you...' What does that mean? It means that we must give ourselves completely, unreservedly to Christ and allow him to take absolute control of our lives. Thus we become partakers of Christ's divine nature, we are born again. Christ is the link that connects us to God's almighty power and it is his own life that is born in us.

There is another law, the law of faith.

'Have faith in God. Therefore I tell you, whatever you ask for in prayer, believe that you have received it, and it will be yours.' Mark 11:22,24.

I began to understand that if I asked with wrong motives my prayer life was hindered.

'When you ask, you do not receive, because you ask with wrong motives, that you may spend what you get on your pleasures.' James 4:3.

A selfish purpose robs prayer of power. We have to learn to pray and be guided in prayer. We need to go into a room and close the door to be alone with God. By shutting the door, we shut out the cares and worries of the world. Wait until you know that you are in the presence of God before you start to speak, then go forward into the throne room with boldness to receive mercy and grace.

That first encounter with God in the throne room is rather terrifying and humbling, knowing that he is almighty, all powerful, God only wise, but also a God of abounding love. To the Christian he is a loving father. We should look up to him to send his Holy Spirit to teach us how to pray.

I remember when I was first married and was in business, I used to worry about everything. One time we ordered a large quantity of material but when it arrived, through a mistake that often happens in business, there was double the quantity we had ordered. The draft was twice what we had budgeted for. The banks had closed down on extra overdraft and I was worried out of my mind about where this money was coming from. That night when we went to bed it was only a short time before John was snoring his head off and I was counting sheep trying to sleep.

In the morning I said to him, 'I didn't sleep a wink last night, but you ... how could you? You snored the whole night through.'

'Oh,' he said, 'I knew that you were worrying about it, so it was no use me worrying about it as well.'

I've had my own back on this one. He said to me later, on another day, 'How is it that you don't worry about things like you used to?'

I said, 'God worries about my problems for me, so there's no need for me to worry too.'

Our prayers should be constant and persistent. I learnt this wonderful truth from my cocker spaniel. When I have a cup of tea with a biscuit, he sits in front of me gazing longingly into my face. I take no notice so he nudges me with his nose and he keeps on until I give him a piece. If I have my heart touched by the persistency of a little dog wanting to be fed, surely my Heavenly Father who is perfect will give me food for my soul.

Here is a practical way of leading a life of prayer. Wait on the Lord every morning, rising early before the rest of the household is up, and ask him for strength, knowledge, wisdom, ability, health and above all love. Then commit your day and yourself into his care, giving thanks and acting as though you have received all that you have asked for.

On retiring at night talk over the things of the day, your weaknesses, your faults that you thought nobody knew about. Tell him that you're incapable of overcoming them, place them in his hands and you will find as the days go by, that you'll become conscious of his guiding hand on you. Ask for the cleansing of your character because you cannot live a powerful prayerful life if you have sin in your heart.

'If I had cherished sin in my heart, the Lord would not have listened.' Psalm 66:18.

Hold short accounts with God and clean everything off the ledger every night and you'll find before long that you'll agree with the writer of the old hymn, 'What a Friend we have in Jesus'.

'Oh, what peace we often forfeit,
Oh, what needless pain we bear,
All because we do not carry
everything to God in prayer.'

17

Growth in our Spiritual Life

I often hear people say, 'What a lovely spiritual life Mrs. So and So lives. But, of course that kind of life isn't for everybody. I couldn't possibly be like that - it's not in my nature.' That isn't what God says. He says that it's for everybody.

There are two gardeners. One is very keen and loves flowers. She purchases a packet of seeds and goes home to prepare the ground with loving care. First she digs it over, then breaks up all the large pieces. She rakes it, manures it, and when the moon is in the right quarter, she sows the seed, and as all good gardeners do, she says, 'God bless you, grow.'

She makes certain that the bed is watered daily so that the tiny seeds will germinate. In about ten days the little seedlings pop their heads out and it's a thrill for the gardener to tend these tiny plants. When they're large enough, they're transplanted to a bed outside where they're exposed a little more to the elements, but are still under the gardener's care.

Soon the plants grow tall and tiny buds appear. The gardener waters through the dry period to make sure of good flowers. Then the flower unfolds and the gardener sees the perfection of something that no human can make. The colour, the shape of the tiny petals and the perfume are like a breath from heaven.

Then we have the other lady who wants to grow flowers, but

somehow she can't get anything to grow. She takes another packet of seeds from the same shelf as the first gardener, goes out and digs a plot in the garden, scatters the seed, rakes over the big clods of soil and goes inside - 'a good job done,' she thinks. She looks on the packet which reads, 'Will germinate in ten days.' She marks the day on her calendar and forgets about the plants.

In ten days she goes out to look. Nothing! What a disappointment! 'I just can't understand why Mrs. Smith gets such good results and I can't get a darn thing - oh well, I suppose she has green fingers!' she says to herself.

The same applies to two types of people. One is a Christian under the tender care of the Heavenly Gardener. She grows by prayer, meditation, study of the Word and spiritual exercise. She blossoms forth in the new life, depending entirely on the Spiritual Gardener for living water. The seeds form and as she goes to and fro, they fall here and there, until finally the last seed is sown. Then the Heavenly Gardener plucks the flower, putting it in his kingdom for eternity.

The other person received the seed of new life, but for lack of spiritual food and water and the choking clods of the world, was stunted and did not bear any seed. She was no good to the Heavenly Gardener, so he cast her away with the weeds.

Don't let the seed of new life lie dormant for lack of spiritual food and water and be stunted for lack of spiritual exercise. Be sure you go to the Heavenly Gardener every day in prayer, Bible reading and meditation, so that your new life can flourish and be a blessing to those around you.

Wisdom is the right use of knowledge. A foolish person is one who has knowledge, but doesn't use it.

King Solomon was noted for his great wisdom. In a dream God appeared to him and said, 'Ask for whatever you want me to give you.'

Solomon had just become king and was aware of his inability to rule wisely, so he said, 'Give your servant a discerning heart to govern your people and to distinguish between right and wrong.'

God answered,

'Since you have asked for this and not for long life or wealth for yourself, I will do what you have asked. I will give you a wise and discerning heart.' 1 Kings 3:5-12.

In the Book of Proverbs, written by Solomon, it says,

'For the Lord gives wisdom, and from his mouth come knowledge and understanding.' Proverbs 2:6.

He also tells us to seek after knowledge, understanding and wisdom as we would seek after silver and treasure.

Today knowledge is increasing throughout the world. This has been made possible by people, through study and research, receiving knowledge, understanding it, and putting it into action.

And millions of people today know that Jesus the Son of God was born into this world. It's a known fact that he died on the cross of Calvary so that our sins can be forgiven. It's a known fact that he rose from the grave victorious over death, and that if we ask his forgiveness for our sins and make him Lord of our lives, he will give us a new life by his Spirit who will dwell in us. It's also a known fact that the Christian has a High Priest, Jesus Christ, the Son of God, who lives forever, speaking to God on our behalf and who is able to save us if we come to God through him.

Do you have this knowledge? All this is vital, but do we understand what it means? These facts are for you personally. Study them until you understand that this sacrifice was made for you because God loves you.

With this knowledge and understanding let us have wisdom. Wisdom is action - of believing the knowledge of what Jesus has done and is still doing for us at God's right hand, and of making it our own by faith.

'Without faith it is impossible to please God, because anyone who comes to him must believe that he exists and that he rewards those who earnestly seek him.' Hebrews 11:6.

What is the difference between a Christian and a non-Christian?

When speaking at a meeting on one occasion I made a call for any that had not accepted Jesus Christ as their saviour to come forward to make their decision.

At the end of the meeting, two young ladies came to me and said that they had never made this decision and didn't think it was necessary. When I asked them why, they replied that they were just as good as any of the church women.

That statement was correct in as much as they were the *same* as the church women. God tells us,

'All people have sinned and fall short of the glory of God.' Romans 3:23.

The difference is that Christian women have become aware of their sinfulness; they have confessed their sins to the one and only sin bearer, Jesus Christ; they have asked for his forgiveness and have been cleansed from all guilt of sin by the blood of Jesus Christ, which was shed expressly for the forgiveness of sin.

It's obvious, with the millions of dollars spent every year on beauty treatments and cosmetics, that women are always searching for ways to improve their physical beauty.

It is just as obvious, with the empty chairs in church, that they are not searching for ways to *inner* beauty for themselves and their families.

There are so many spiritual lessons that we can learn from ordinary things that we accept as part of every day life.

Our 'Friendship Group' had a cosmetics demonstration and the beautician produced from a box all that she needed. First she showed us a magnifying mirror, saying that this was to reveal any defects in the skin. Next came the cleansing lotion. She explained that before attempting treatment for skin blemishes, the skin must be thoroughly cleansed. Treatment must start from the base of the skin. The astringent was then applied which closed the pores so that dirt and germs could not attack again. This acts as protection. It also stings in any places where there are blemishes. Then the cosmetics were applied and the natural beauty of the model was enhanced.

I too am a beautician, but in a different way. All I need for my demonstration is the Holy Bible. First I want to introduce you to Jesus Christ. He is the magnifying mirror of our inner selves, of our characters. Blemishes show up when we look at him face to face. Then we have the cleansing. His blood was shed for the cleansing of blemishes caused by sin, and as we apply his blood through faith, our blemished natures are made clean. Then we have Jesus as the restorer. In his own words he says, 'I am making everything new!' (Revelation 21:5). He restores our characters to health and beauty.

The fruit of the Spirit, love, joy, peace, patience, kindness, goodness, faithfulness, gentleness and self-control are then applied and added to our characters so we have beauty indeed.

18

The Decision is Yours

What has humankind got to offer the world today - mass murder, ethnic cleansing, genocide?

What has Christ to offer the world today? To each individual who takes him as Lord and King, he offers a brand new life, love, freedom, security, and equality. He offers restoration and health personally and in our relationships. He will lead all to the knowledge of truth. Christ's kingdom is in the hearts of men and women, and where Christ is, social orders will be put right.

Don't let us make the same mistake as those of 33 A.D. Don't let us yell with the crowd 'crucify him!' and put him away without a fair trial. Give him what fair-minded citizens expect for themselves. Give him a fair trial in your life and heart before you condemn him.

From the days when God closed the gates of the Garden of Eden and pronounced he would send a saviour into the world, born of a woman, it was the desire, as each woman conceived, that she would be the chosen one. Christ came to give us new life, peace and unity. Since the time he ascended into heaven, the gift of the Holy Spirit has been given to his people - to each man and woman, and we have the honour of bringing Christ afresh into the world with each heart that is surrendered to God.

The price of unity and peace is sacrifice and love. Because of Mary's obedience, Christ entered the world. When Mary received the news from God's messenger, she didn't say, 'It's impossible', although she thought it improbable. By faith she accepted the message as true.

People say, 'I admire his faith,' or 'I wish I had her faith.' Some say they have given themselves to the Lord but don't feel any different. Faith is not a matter of feeling. Faith is born out of our confidence in God. You are absolutely sure that the statements that God makes are true, therefore you act accordingly. If your faith is weak, begin to learn more about Christ.

Some people can go through life playing hunches, but not me. I'm no gambler, I place my confidence only in a sure thing, something or someone I've tried and found to be all that it or they claim to be.

But although our faith cannot be based on feelings, feelings cannot be divorced from Christ. It is the feeling of guilt and the feeling of hopelessness in our lives as sinners that makes us search and turn to Christ. We repent with the feeling of sorrow for what we have done or left undone, then there is the feeling of joy and assurance when your spirit and God's Spirit come together in fellowship.

Let our faith be practical, and when we know what God would have us do, let us go ahead and do it no matter how puny our efforts may seem. A tiny effort blessed by God may be the means of bringing salvation to many.

I am no speaker. I am no teacher. I am no writer. Why don't I scrap my efforts and leave it to someone else? But it is by faith that I seek to live, believing that God will fulfil his purpose in and through me. The sticks on the altar of sacrifice, having been set, can be set alight with fire from above.

PART TWO
INVOLVEMENT WITH GOD

Involvement with God

We're already involved up to our necks in work, family needs and problems. One more involvement would be the last straw to break our backs and our spirits. But involvement with God is something different. It doesn't add weight but instead brings relief. Involvement with God is the answer to living - not existing - LIVING.

Perhaps you once had a childhood knowledge of Jesus, but you've so involved yourself with other things that you've had to drop him. You've become lost.

You see, in our involvement with the world, we've never really understood God's involvement with us. God created us, he made us and he breathed his spirit into us to give us life. He knows our every thought, word and action and sees us as no one else does, as we really are. He sees into our very souls and knows the motives that urge us to act the way we do.

Because we lack God's power, purpose and peace in our lives, we flutter between involvements trying to find satisfaction, but it always evades us. God knows every move we make and patiently waits for us to admit that we've had enough.

'Do you not know? Have you not heard? The Lord is the everlasting God, the Creator of the ends of the earth. He will not grow tired or weary, and his understanding no one can fathom. He gives strength to the weary and increases the power of the weak.' Isaiah 40:28,29.

If God knows what kind of person I am, what could he possibly want to do with me?

We are inclined to think of sin as crime - sin against the law, and moral sin which is sin against ourselves - but it is more than that. My Bible Concordance says, 'Sin is any thought, word, action, omission or desire, contrary to the law of God.' The original sin was rebellion against God from which all other sins stem.

Because of God's love and his involvement with us, he sent his Son, Jesus Christ, to take the punishment for our sin, so that we may come back into the family of God, and under his guidance, be the kind of people he wants us to be - the kind of people we would like to be, but find it impossible to become. How could God possibly love a person like me?

A mother of twelve children was once asked which of her children she loved the most. She replied, 'The one who is sick until better; the one who is crying until smiling; the one who is lost until found.' Being a mother I can understand that perfectly, and that is just what God is like.

When I saw God as a parent, I saw his message to me in a new way. The first fact in my relationship with God is that I've missed the mark and missed out without him.

One day I had a practical demonstration of this. I was using an electric polishing machine on my kitchen floor when it suddenly stopped. I checked for a power failure but found other appliances still operating. Then I checked the polishing machine and found that the cord bringing the power into the machine had worked loose. Without power the machine was useless. As I stood looking at it a wonderful truth came to me.

When this machine was designed, it was made to operate on electric power and nothing else could take that place. So that the polishing machine could function properly again, I had to push the plug back into place, and then the machine worked perfectly. The power was there all the time, but careless handling of the machine caused the stoppage.

When God made me, I was designed to be controlled by his power, and nothing else could take his place. Careless handling of our own lives stops the power of God flowing into us, and it is only the Lord Jesus Christ, the mediator, or connecting cord, who can bring this power back into our lives.

'For there is one God and one mediator between God and men, the man Christ Jesus.' 1 Timothy 2:5.

Nobody is truly self-sufficient. If our confidence is in humanity, our confidence is a very frail thing. Our sufficiency must come from the power of God, and we can have this power if we're prepared to be involved with Christ.

'To all who received him, to those who believed in his name, he gave the right to become children of God...' John 1:12.

You see the power is there all the time available to all, but only those who receive the Lord Jesus Christ as their saviour will receive the power.

Cleansing

One day I placed a piece of red lining material into straight bleach in a saucer and then went away for about fifteen minutes. When I came back I found that the colour had been taken out completely, leaving the material a cream colour.

If you have something that is soiled or stained, the stained object has to be immersed in cleansing or bleaching fluid. If we haven't experienced the joy and peace that comes with forgiveness of sins, we haven't followed the directions. God has promised a complete 'change of colour' to our hearts.

> *'Come now, let us reason together,' says the Lord. 'Though your sins are like scarlet, they shall be as white as snow; though they are red as crimson, they shall be like wool.'* Isaiah 1:18.

The cleansing agent is the blood of Jesus Christ, that is, the sacrifice of Christ on the cross.

> *'...and the blood of Jesus, his Son, purifies us from all sin'.* 1 John 1:7.

Total Surrender

I remember quite clearly saying in a prayer, 'I'll do anything for you Lord, except speak at Women's Meetings.' I wanted to pick and choose as I'd always done. To be honest, I was just plain scared. I'd never spoken at a women's meeting of any kind, and certainly never about Jesus Christ. I was afraid of ridicule, criticism and gossip.

It wasn't long after this that John and I decided to take our girls to the Waitomo Caves to see the glow worms. We stayed at the Waitomo Hotel and spent two days exploring the caves and the country round about. The magnificence of the caves was overwhelming, while the uniqueness of the underground lake intrigued us.

Tied to a jetty in the cave was a large dinghy that we all boarded. Everyone was told to be very quiet and the dinghy glided silently out into the middle of the lake. As we glanced up at the roof of the cave which was exceedingly high, a myriad of tiny lights came into view

What a sight, what delicate beauty, and we started to whisper among ourselves. The attendant told us to shout, which we all did. The roof went completely black. The attendant guided the boat back again and told us that it would be a little while before the glow worms would shine again. There was no way we could have harmed the glow worms, but the noise put out their lights.

Jesus said to his followers,

'You are the light of the world. A city on a hill cannot be hidden. Neither do people light a lamp and put it under a bowl. Instead they put it on its stand, and it gives light to everyone in the house. In the same way, let your light shine before men, that they may see your good deeds and praise your Father in heaven.' Matthew 5:14-16.

Being of a nervous temperament, I can't say that I enjoyed the days of preparation to speak at meetings or the actual delivery of the message, but I depended on God and the peace and glow of obedience that followed kept my light shining.

For our Good

The fact that God always desires to give good things seems to elude us. We've built into ourselves a fear that if we come too near to God we'll be made slaves. We're afraid of what he might ask us to do.

When they were children, my daughters loved to lick the basin and beaters once I had finished making a cake. I would usually call out, 'Does anyone want the beaters and basin?' There was always a race to see who could get there first. But one day, when I'd finished the cake,

I called them without telling them what I had, and received no reply. I called again and there was still no reply, so I washed the basin and beaters. It wasn't long before they came into the kitchen and saw the clean utensils.

'Have you finished making the cake?' they asked.

'Yes.' I said.

'But you've washed the basin and the beaters!'

'Yes,' I replied, 'I called, but you didn't answer. You heard me, didn't you?'

'Yes,' they said, 'but we thought you wanted us to do something for you.'

I know many of us turn a deaf ear to God's calling because we think we may have to do something for him. We go through life ignoring his call only because we haven't realised the wonderful truth from his Word.

'No good thing does he withhold from those whose walk is blameless. O Lord Almighty, blessed is the man who trusts in you.' Psalm 84:11,12.

God's will for us is 'good, pleasing and perfect' (Romans 12:2). Do we really believe in God's loving heart?

Before I understood these words, there were numerous times when I was rebellious in circumstances that cropped up in my life. As time went on I learnt why things had to happen to me. God was transferring my dependence on material things, people and myself, to dependence entirely on him. Now I can honestly say that I believe God's will for us is good, perfect and pleasing.

New Life

We know that we have free choice about our involvements, but Jesus Christ says, 'choose life'. What good are our involvements unless we have life?

People often refer to life as a rat race. They're going round in circles chasing their tails. They get up in the morning to go to work to earn money to buy the food to give them strength to get up in the morning to go to work to buy the food... We have a choice. We can stay in the rat race or choose a new way.

I went to see a friend of mine one day and found her doing the washing. She was in a little shed outside, a 'copper' boiling furiously, and the room full of steam and smoke. She was bent over a wooden tub with a washboard that she was scrubbing clothes on.

'You ought to buy a washing machine,' I said, knowing perfectly well that she could afford it.

She said, 'What do I want with a washing machine? I've been doing the washing like this for twenty years.'

I told her that a machine could relieve her of some of the burden of washing, but she was pretty stubborn. She clung to her argument that if she had done the washing this way for twenty years she could go on doing it for another twenty.

But I had put a new thought in her mind and within a month she asked me to recommend a good washing machine. She bought the machine, was thrilled with its performance and said that she didn't know how she had managed so long without it.

If we accept Christ's invitation to come to him for new life, he will help to carry our burdens, and we too will wonder how we managed so long without him.

Involvement with Other People

It was ten o'clock on a drizzling winter night when I was driving hom
From a picture theatre on my right, a little boy dressed in dark gr
came running out. He didn't stop to look left or right but just ran straig
out onto the road where an on-coming car caught him with its rig
mudguard and flung him into the middle of the road. I was so shak
by what I'd seen that I pulled up to the kerb and just sat.

The motorist took the boy into a shop close by and rang for an ar
bulance. Then he came out and began talking to a small group that h
gathered. As he spoke to them they started to walk away and I cou
see that nobody wanted to help. I got out of my car and went across tl
road towards him. Just then, two other men came along and one said
him, 'You motorists are all the same, you're always speeding.' That fal
accusation was all I needed. I looked into the motorist's distressed whi
face and said, 'I saw what happened. I'll be a witness for you.'

He caught hold of my arm and said with tears in his eyes, 'Than
God for you, lady.' My natural tendency as I sat in the car was to st
put and not get involved, but Christ compelled involvement.

A few nights later a policeman came to get a statement from me ar
he said, 'Mrs Mitchell, it's most unusual for a stranger to offer to be
witness.'

'Why?' I said.

'People don't want to be involved with things like this. It takes ι
too much of their time,' he answered.

This is our natural reaction, but Jesus Christ says in the story of tl
Good Samaritan that involvement with another in need is the only qua
fication for being a good neighbour.

Do we see pain and distress among our neighbours or among those of other countries and ignore them? Involvement with Christ demands involvement with our neighbours and all humanity.

Testimony and Witnessing

Some people say that they have no testimony because they've come from Christian families and have grown up in church life, that they've always been Christians.

Regular church attendance is commendable, but there's a grave danger. We are subject to habits. Good habits are just as hard to give up as bad habits. You can ask an elderly man why he gets up at six o'clock every morning and reads the newspaper when he has all day to do this. He'll say, 'I don't know. When I was young I got into the habit and I've always done it.'

Likewise with the man who goes to the hotel every night to drink with his mates. He doesn't know why, but it's become a habit.

Going to church or involving yourself in church affairs can become a good habit, but it's the acceptance of Jesus Christ as personal Saviour that gives testimony for witnessing.

Others have difficulty in witnessing because their experience of Jesus Christ was unspectacular or undramatic. Perhaps they opened their hearts and received him in a very quiet way, but Jesus Christ has become a living reality in their lives just the same. Don't be afraid to share your experience with others whether it was quiet or spectacular. God uses both to influence other lives to take the same step.

A spectacular experience of Christ can be a dangerous thing if our witnessing depends solely upon our past experience. We'll soon find it becoming less effective as time passes. Our experience, testimony and witness can only be maintained by constantly feeding on the Word of God and by looking continually to him who is the same yesterday, today and forever.

It has been said that some people are so heavenly minded that they are no earthly use, but don't let that be said about us.

One of our jobs as women is to be homemakers. The kind of home we make, is what we have to live in. If our home is built on suspicion, jealousy, hate, greed and self-indulgence, we've built a hell for ourselves. But if our home is built on love, which is supplied by the Holy Spirit filling the human heart, we'll have peace, joy, patience, self control, humility and love: a corner of heaven.

A busy woman may never witness in front of a crowded church, but her life and work can speak volumes.

I want to quote the thirty-first chapter of Proverbs in its entirety from verse ten:

'A wife of noble character who can find? She is worth far more than rubies. Her husband has full confidence in her and lacks nothing of value. She brings him good, not harm, all the days of her life. She selects wool and flax and works with eager hands. She is like the merchant ships, bringing her food from afar. She gets up while it is still dark; she provides food for her family and portions for her servant girls. She considers a field and buys it; out of her earnings she plants a vineyard. She sets about her work vigorously; her arms are strong for her tasks. She sees that her trading is profitable, and her lamp does not go out at night. In her hand she holds the distaff and grasps the spindle with her fingers. She opens her arms to the poor and extends her hands to the needy. When it snows, she has no fear for her household; for all of them are clothed in scarlet. She makes coverings for her

bed; she is clothed in fine linen and purple. Her husband is respected at the city gate, where he takes his seat among the elders of the land. She makes linen garments and sells them, and supplies the merchants with sashes. She is clothed with strength and dignity; she can laugh at the days to come. She speaks with wisdom, and faithful instruction is on her tongue. She watches over the affairs of her household and does not eat the bread of idleness. Her children arise and call her blessed; her husband also, and he praises her: 'Many women do noble things, but you surpass them all.' Charm is deceptive, and beauty is fleeting; but a woman who fears the Lord is to be praised. Give her the reward she has earned, and let her works bring her praise at the city gate.'

Take heart, for you're in the place where God would have you be.

Sustained Fervour

One day I was asked by my minister to take the morning service at church, and was prompted by God to speak about cleansing. So I got out the bottle of bleach and the material to take with me. As I looked at the material I saw that it had been screwed up in the bottom of a bag, so I put the iron on. When I put the hot iron on the material it changed colour. It was too late to do anything about it then, but when I got to the church I found that the colour had gone back to normal. Again I saw that God was teaching me another wonderful lesson.

There are times when a church makes a special one-off effort to tell people outside the church about Christ. Everyone is enthusiastic. They pitch in with the arrangements, visit neighbours and arrange transport, but as soon as the mission is over they go back into the same old rut. During a mission, the minister or missioner starts to apply the heat by challenging and encouraging the people towards a greater effort and we all change colour. As soon as the mission is over and the 'heat' is lifted a little we go back into retirement.

> *'Never be lacking in zeal, but keep your spiritual fervour, serving the Lord.'* Romans 12:11.

Being 'Salt'

Patterns of life keep changing. When my children were very young, I needed live-in help so that I would be able to continue with my social involvements. I mentioned this to my sister who had connections with an organisation that cared for unmarried mothers and the adoption of their babies. She asked me if I would consider taking one of these girls for three months to help out the organisation. After talking it over with my husband, we decided to give it a try - I needed help and so did the girl, so it worked well.

For the next six years, twenty-one girls came to live with us. These girls were lovely looking, the majority between sixteen and eighteen years old. With about one exception, I would have loved to have had them as my own daughters.

I met the mothers and fathers when they brought their daughters. The parents were always astounded at what had happened; they felt disgraced in front of their neighbours and friends; they were deeply hurt that their daughters had done such a thing to them. One, crying, said to me, 'Where did I fail her?' I couldn't answer at the time, but can now.

After receiving these girls for four years, I became a Christian, and tried to tell them about Christ and his salvation, forgiveness of sins and a start again in a new life. I was soon to learn that their experience had caused more than just a physical change. There was hate and resentment. Resentment that 'he' had got off 'scot-free' and that they were left to go through it alone. There was such hate that some said that they could easily and cheerfully strangle the boys if they could get their hands on them.

I know that salt must be added to a meal while it's cooking to obtain the best flavour. If you've forgotten to salt the porridge or potatoes and try adding it when they are on the plate, it's noticeable straight away.

Salt is what we are. It's no use having salt but not adding it. As salt, I knew that I had to become involved with the people around us, involved with young lives growing up, teaching them about Christ, the Living Bread, as they grew to maturity.

I was converted when my eldest daughter was five years old, and the promise I had made to God at her christening came back to me. I knew I had to take her to Sunday School and go to church myself. I took a Bible Class while she went to Sunday School. Instead of Sunday being for sports and a holiday, it became a teaching and rest day, and I attended the evening service.

As the years passed, I had the wonderful privilege of teaching my own daughter in Bible Class. When she was fourteen she told me that she wanted to give her life to Jesus. A change takes place in a young life that has been 'salted' since birth. Before she gave her life to Christ, any old thing would do for her school work. It didn't matter if it was her best or not, just so long as she had something to take to school. After receiving Christ, a change took place. She took a lot longer over her homework and the light wouldn't go out until ten o'clock. When I went in to say goodnight, it would be her Bible and Bible notes that kept her up and not comics as before. I asked her why she was working so hard, and she said that she had to do her best so that God would be able to use her.

We have a wonderful fellowship together and one day she said to me with a lot of feeling in her voice, 'Mum, I'm glad you're a Christian, because if you hadn't told me I would never have known.'

If more mothers would be salt to their children, perhaps we could save young people from the destruction of drugs and immorality.

'Salting' the young is a privilege that gives great joy.

Freedom, Satisfaction and Purpose

In my grandfather's day the rule was that the young generation should be seen and not heard. Today they have freedom to express themselves, often to the despair of Mum and Dad! Stereos blare all day; TV on all night; 'boy-racers' drive up and down the road; teenagers come and go at all hours of the day and night; drink, drugs and sexual involvement - all used to find some kind of meaning in life. Their expression is created through music with a solid beat. They shout their message with straining voices.

Their actions, manner, despondent faces and eyes scream, 'WE ARE SICK AND LOST.' The music plays on and the distressed voices call through their own songs, 'Who will answer, who will answer to our needs? Where will we find acceptance?' And God says, 'I will hear them.'

'The Lord is near to all who call on him, to all who call on him in truth. He fulfils the desires of those who fear him; he hears their cry and saves them. The Lord watches over all who love him, but all the wicked he will destroy.' Psalm 145:18-20.

Our young people have their freedom, but unless freedom is linked with responsibility and purpose, satisfaction will always evade them. Freedom without guidance and knowledge can bring destruction and death.

As parents, how can we help our young people? Is it more education they require? Is it more community centres and sports fields? Better homes and clothes? Is it still more freedom? What else can there possibly be?

Young people have the tendency of withdrawing from the world to live in a world of their own creation. There is too much pain and too many restrictions, too many 'do's' and 'don'ts', and they can't cope with them.

God took care of this problem when he sent Jesus Christ into the world. Jesus loves us, accepts us, heals us, gives us a reason to live, and gives us the power and strength to carry on.

Just as a lack of minerals in pasture soil can cause healthy animals to become sick and die, so it will be with our children if we let them go into the wide world without Jesus Christ as their strength to overcome all the temptations that they face.

God said to Paul,

'My grace is sufficient for you, for my power is made perfect in weakness.' 2 Corinthians 12:9.

Can we tell our children about our experience of God's power and strength?

We can present Jesus Christ to them. Let us confess our weakness then trust in the grace and love of God.

Discipline

When I was a new Christian I used to call older Christians 'fuddy-duddys' and couldn't understand why everything worked so slowly. Then one day, on the road to Rotorua, I learnt one of the greatest lessons of my Christian life.

We were driving along and, as we turned a corner, right in front of us was a tremendous flock of sheep. Men idled along on horses and dogs kept the flock together. Knowing that it was going to take us a long time to get through, I stepped out of the car and started to walk in front to clear a path. I noticed that with the drover, there was a young sheep dog with its front paw through its collar. Being a dog lover I was horrified and said to the man, 'Why have you put this dog's paw through its collar?'

He said, 'Lady, this is a young dog being trained for the job. If he was allowed to run with the other dogs, in his excitement and inexperience he would scatter the flock. In a couple of weeks he'll be allowed to run with them.'

The other dogs were way out in front, but the master kept this little dog by his side. The master had a purpose for him.

Perhaps in all our Christian experience, the Master may never be so close to us as he is in that frustrating period of studying, of being grounded in the Bible and learning the art of praying, when we would rather be more active in our Father's business. To be given a place in God's work is surely the greatest privilege and cannot be taken lightly. It's by prayer that we get to know God and his will for us. It's by patience that we learn to follow his lead. It's by constant study of the Word of God that we're trained in obedience.

Sharing

Conversion is a private matter between God and the individual, and many people don't like to talk about such an intimate experience. These were my feelings on the matter, although God had commissioned me to write. Realising that I wouldn't get any peace until I had written my experiences down, I did so and put them safely away in a box.

But one day, a lady from 'The Challenge', a Christian newspaper, rang to ask me if I would write my testimony for her. She told me that if I'd give it to her directly it would save her having to go to one of my meetings and report it. Knowing that reporters don't always report words correctly, I agreed to give her the work I'd done.

From that day on I became involved with a real out and out Christian. I'd been willing to coast along in the good old New Zealand 'she's right' way, but after having met Mrs Grace Shaw, the Challenge reporter, a woman with a deep concern for the spiritual life of other women, I knew I couldn't withhold my message any longer.

At first I was afraid that if I spoke about my experience I'd have nothing left for myself. It was a great comfort to have it tucked away. But as I wrote and spoke to other women about my conversion and spiritual experiences, I found the same principle operating as for the poor widow who fed Elijah with the oil and meal. Like her, when I shared what God had given me, I found my own spiritual resources multiplied.

From this, a small band of women decided to get together and do something about sharing with their neighbours. About half were converts from the Billy Graham Crusade held in Auckland in 1959. They decided to have a coffee hour in a private home, and invite their friends and neighbours so they could talk about what knowing Christ and receiving him into their lives had done for them. At the first coffee hour, about twenty-five people attended. Subsequent coffee hours grew until, within a year, a Municipal Hall was hired to take the 400 attendees. As women from other districts saw the possibilities, they also started coffee hours in their homes until they too had to use halls to accommodate the people.

This form of sharing wasn't a new idea. In the Bible we read about a woman called Lydia who was converted through Paul's preaching. She was a business woman going about her own affairs, but as soon as she received the gospel of Christ she opened her home to share her new faith with her friends and neighbours in a practical way.

Action

Some years after I became a Christian, and my husband John was convinced that Christianity was no flash in the pan, I asked him what he thought about me when I first took Jesus Christ as my Saviour. He said, 'I knew you had something. You took off like a jet.'

Christian life can be likened to jet travel. You want to travel so you go to the airport for departure. Once airborne, you leave your home and those you love behind.

In plane travel, when the navigator plots the course, there is always a place marked on the map as 'the point of no return'.

When the pilot boards the plane, he is given the O.K. for take-off. For me, this is always a slightly anxious but thrilling moment. The engines roar and the plane moves slowly at first until it gathers momentum to take-off speed. The wheels leave the ground and immediately the sensation of high speed settles into a comfortable motion. To be a Christian, you first decide to change your old way of life and are then prepared to do something about it. Jesus Christ is your means of transport, and faith in his ability to get you safely to your destination is the fuel needed for your journey. Your journey is made alone and your faith seems frail for the colossal journey ahead. Contact is made with God through his Word, and information and instructions are given by his Holy Spirit.

The take-off, or moment of commitment, is a moment of thrill and anxiety, because by nature we are earthbound. It's not easy to give up temporal things for a promise of something better. We certainly cannot take-off by our own power. Unbelief is like gravity that holds us down.

After initially committing my life in trust to God, I wanted to go on in the Christian life, but I hadn't taken off. Then a wonderful thought came to me from God. 'Why do you still keep asking for something that has been given to you? I am your strength, knowledge, wisdom, ability, health and love. Claim and take what you require.' I put out my hand to Jesus Christ and touched him by faith. With this thrust of faith, the grips of doubt were released, and I was on my way past the point of no return. There is no going back when there is nowhere else to go.

Completeness

I've found in Christ the fulfilment of my soul's desire. Jesus had spoken to me through the Bible in a way that I could understand. As he became a reality in my life, he also became a necessity.

Through the verses of the Bible which begin with the words 'I AM', God made me aware of my need of him.

'I AM THE VINE; you are the branches. If a man remains in me and I in him, he will bear much fruit; apart from me you can do nothing.' John15:5.

To make a practical demonstration of this parable, I took a piece of cardboard and taped to it a leaf I had cut from a healthy vine growing in my home. By the next day the leaf was already dying. For the next few weeks, I repeated the process until I had six leaves on the card. By this time the first leaf was so withered and dry that it was brittle, and each consecutive leaf was going through the stages that would ultimately bring about the same condition. They were no use for anything but to be burnt. The leaves still on the vine were vigorous and healthy.

From this parable I learnt the importance of being attached to Jesus Christ to receive life - without him I can do nothing. Living without him is useless, like the leaves that were separated from the vine.

'*I AM THE BREAD OF LIFE.*' John 6:35.

We don't realise how important bread is to us until the bakers go on strike. No matter what we use it can't take the place of bread, and our appetites aren't entirely satisfied. Fresh bread has to be eaten on the day it's baked to be enjoyed at its best, and Christ the Bread of Life must also be taken fresh every day. This requires a personal involvement with him.

'*Man does not live on bread alone, but on every word that comes from the mouth of God.*' Matthew 4:4.

Just as I need food every day, I also need contact with God through his Word and by prayer.

'*I AM THE TRUTH.*' John 14:6.

Books, magazines and literature of all descriptions make a great impact on our lives every day. Because of conflicting opinions it is sometimes difficult to know the 'truth'. Fantasy and romance are portrayed as truth, and many are disillusioned when they find that the results promised have evaded them.

I can trust Jesus Christ because he is the TRUTH. I can believe his words and promises and act on them.

'I AM THE GOOD SHEPHERD.' John 10:11.

A good shepherd is one who devotes his life to the care and wellbeing of his flock. He is also the guardian of the sheep to see that none are lost and to care for them when they are sick.

As a mother, I realise how important it is for children to have someone to care for them, to keep them from danger and to make a home where they're free from anxiety.

Because I've become a member of God's family, I can enjoy those privileges. I can rely on the Good Shepherd and all he stands for.

'I AM THE LIGHT.' John 8:12.

I looked up my Bible Concordance to see what the Bible has to say about light. I found the word mentioned as a noun over eighty times in the Old Testament, and over fifty times in the New Testament. In 1 Kings 11:36 light is referred to as the son or successor that keeps a person's name and memory from being extinguished.

It is referred to as a window, true saving knowledge, happiness and prosperity, support, comfort and deliverance. It refers to Jesus Christ as the fountain and author of all knowledge, both natural and spiritual, of the Word of God that conducts and guides Christians in this world, and points out the way of eternal happiness.

One of the most annoying experiences is to find yourself suddenly plunged into darkness when making dinner. After finding the matches, you rummage through the drawers to find a candle or torch, and tempers get frayed. What a wonderful relief it is when the lights come on again and you can see what you're doing and where you're going. This is the result we can expect in our lives when Jesus Christ, who is the Light, illuminates us.

'I AM THE WAY.' John 14:6.

There are many different ways that can be taken in this life, but Jesus Christ is the only one to say truthfully, 'I am *the* way.'

Have you ever experienced the feeling of being lost on a country road? Deep within yourself you know that somewhere you must have taken a wrong turn, uneasiness and doubt keeps flooding your mind. There's only one sensible thing to do, and that's to ask somebody who knows the way to give you directions.

Be assured that Jesus Christ, who is the way, will guide you through life if only you'll ask and commit yourself in faith to him.

'I AM THE DOOR.' John 10:9.

There seems to be a great fear in many of going through this door. They seem to think that, if they go through, the door will slam and they'll become prisoners. It's not until we go through the door and receive our *freedom* that we realise we have, in fact, been prisoners and slaves all our lives. 'I am the door,' says Jesus Christ.

'Whoever enters through me will be saved. He will come in and go out, and find pasture.' John 10:9.

Through this door we not only find freedom and satisfaction but purpose - God's purpose for our lives, as we enter a new dimension of living.

Believing

'Without faith it is impossible to please God, because anyone who comes to him must believe that he exists and that he rewards those who earnestly seek him.' Hebrews 11:6.

How can I believe? I can't see, feel, hear, taste or smell God, so how am I to believe if I'm not made aware of him through my five senses?

Belief in God is a matter of contract. He has given us his side of the contract in the New Testament, revealed by and through his Son, the Lord Jesus Christ. It's true that we can't know him completely through our five senses, but the very nature of God is revealed in the life, death and resurrection of Jesus Christ. The love of God for us, as sinful human beings, is seen as we look at the Lord Jesus nailed to the cross to make payment for our sins.

Moses was told that his people were not to come up the mountain with him when he went to talk with God because no man can look on the face of God and live. It's also true that no person can look on the face of Jesus Christ, crucified for them, without dying to self.

This contract with God is a love contract. We give ourselves and all we have to him, in an act of faith, and receive from him, in return, himself and all he has. It's similar to a wedding covenant. Two people sign a marriage contract and both parties go away believing and acting as a married couple. They now have a new status, a new freedom and a new responsibility. This is exactly what happens when we believe God.

Belief is a contract with God that turns into a union, and from this union all other relationships find their rightful place.

When we see the state of the world in which we live, many ask why God doesn't act. But he has already done something. He has intervened in this world in some rather unexpected ways: through the stable in Bethlehem, the carpenter's shop in Nazareth and the cross on Calvary. This wasn't exactly what the people had in mind in those days, but those who believed God went through a tremendous change in their lives and turned the thinking of the world upside down.

Perhaps we're looking for a more spectacular or dramatic intervention by God in the world, but believe me, if you mean business with God, he will intervene in your life and turn your whole world upside down. You'll emerge as a new person with new status, new freedom and new responsibility.

Commitment

Commitment means to 'entrust', 'give charge' or 'make a lasting agreement'. To commit your life to Jesus means that you make a definite decision to entrust your life to him.

So many people think that as long as they try to live a good life and don't do anybody harm, they'll be able to enter the kingdom of God. God's Word says that Jesus is the only way to heaven and that no man can come to God the Father except through him.

Most of us are members of some club, organisation or community group that is governed by a set of rules. It is an accepted fact that unless we are willing to follow these we cannot become members or accept the privileges offered.

Don't make the grave mistake of thinking you can enter God's kingdom on your *own* terms. I tried this for years and got absolutely nowhere. You don't have to wait until you've made your life any better, and you don't have to wait until it's worse.

You can make this commitment now. Say in your own words,

Lord Jesus, I know that I am a sinner, and repent of my sin.

I believe you died on the cross for me and I thank you with all my heart.

By faith I receive you to live in my heart and life as my Lord and Saviour.

I give my heart and my whole life, everything I have, to you. I am prepared, with your help, to tell others about you and by the power of the Holy Spirit live my life dedicated to you. Amen.

PART THREE

FROM STRENGTH TO STRENGTH

From Strength to Strength

It is now forty years since my conversion. During those years, I was often asked when I would write this final part of my story. I was more or less hoping that I wouldn't have to because it's so personal, but there's nothing more frustrating than reading a story to find the end missing.

We hear testimonies from people who have received Jesus Christ in their lives, and about the joy and freedom they've received. Some go on in the Lord's service, others go cold and let the seed of everlasting life die.

Did the glow of my encounter with God and the Holy Spirit snuff out as time went by?

Was the world with all its enticing and the problems that life brings able to shatter my faith?

It would be wonderful if, on making a commitment to Jesus Christ, we could just be taken up out of this world. The freedom, love and joy of proclaiming our faith in him to be our sin bearer, sustainer, guide and lover are so real that we want to be with him.

But God had a long-term plan for me. Conversion was only the first step, my decision to let Jesus Christ take over my life and to let him transform me into the person God would have me be.

The Holy Spirit plants a new 'seed' in the heart of everyone who believes in God and the seed begins to grow. I realised that this isn't a momentary thing but rather an on-going process as God renews the heart and mind of those who believe.

Through the 'Parable of the Sower' (Matthew 13:3-8) Jesus warns us what can happen to the seed. We can hear the Word of God and mentally agree with the message, but if this acceptance is only head knowledge the message is seed that has landed on the surface and gone no deeper.

Or we can hear the message with gladness, but because of a lack of biblical knowledge we become confused, going from church to church seeking the answers from people and moving away from the source of truth that God has placed within us. Or if the seed falls among 'thorns', the bad habits that we can't or won't give up, eventually the seed that has been sown is choked.

The world's standard today is far different from the standards of the world God first created. Material possessions, the stress of this world, riches, power and lust choke the message. These are counterfeits with which Satan has deceived the world. But the fruit of God's Spirit is love, joy, peace, patience, kindness, goodness, faithfulness, gentleness and self-control (Galatians 5:22-23).

I longed that the seed God sowed in my life would be seed sown on good ground. I heard the message and sought to keep the ground fertile with Bible study and prayer. God equipped me to tell others about his love, forgiveness and mercy.

I was very disappointed that John, my husband, hadn't made the same commitment as me. But there was no going back. Life went on as it does in an ordinary family. Nothing had changed except me.

I was invited by the Session of my church to become an elder. Being a woman, this caused me some concern, so I sought advice. It was pointed out to me that there is no male or female to those who are in Christ Jesus. We are new creations, filled with the Spirit of God. I took this up with God in prayer and asked that if it were his will he would see it done.

The month before my ordination, John was having health problems and business stresses, and had come to the end of his tether. One day as I took a cup of tea to him he said, 'Look, I've made a fool of myself. I've left God out of my life. Tell me, how can I become a Christian?'

'Oh John,' I said, 'for the past twelve years I've spoken to you about it.'

'I never heard a word,' he said.

Later that morning he said, 'Let's go to the Waitakere Ranges so that we won't be disturbed.'

We took the short trip to this forest area by car, and I told him the gospel very simply. That morning his heart was soft, not only did he listen, but he also understood.

For my ordination I asked John and my daughters to come to communion and support me. After receiving the 'right hand of fellowship' from the rest of the elders, I was just turning to go back to my seat when the minister told me to wait. He called John to the altar where John gave his life to Jesus Christ! My church family knew that I had been waiting for twelve years and tears of joy flowed among the congregation.

Storms in our Lives

The storms in life make us feel helpless. On one occasion we were cruising on our launch when a terrible storm hit almost without warning and grew worse as the day went on. Although we were in a 'safe' mooring, the wind was roaring overhead and the boat tossed and turned on the anchor like a bucking horse. The storm raged into the night. At about 9.30 p.m. John looked worn out with worry. There was nothing we could do but to sit and listen for the pull of the anchor on the warp.

Eventually I said to John, 'Go to bed, I'll wake you about one o'clock so you can take the second watch.' Goodness knows what I would have done if the boat had started to drag anchor. I just sat there as the boat rose with every wave, waiting for the wrench of the rope as the anchor bit into the sand.

It was nearing midnight, I was tired and exhausted and began to pray desperately, 'Please help me Lord, please help me.' About another half hour went by and I was waiting for the noise of the rope on the anchor when the storm seemed to weaken. By one o'clock the storm had abated so I went to John and said, 'Sleep on, the storm has been taken away.'

I was reminded of the disciples in a storm (Mark 4:35-41). Jesus was asleep in the stern of the boat. They were terrified and called to Jesus, 'Don't you care that we'll perish?'

Jesus got up, rebuked the wind and said to the sea, 'Peace, be still.' Then he said to the disciples, 'Where is your faith?'

The disciples were afraid and they said to one another, 'What kind of man is this? He commands even the winds and the water and they obey him.'

John's passion was the sea and boats, golf and business all in that order. I could see that he was coming under extreme pressure from these things.

While cruising, the following Christmas, we sheltered from a sudden storm in Tryphena harbour in Great Barrier Island. During the night John decided to move the launch to a safer position. Although we had a winch to pull up our anchor, bringing it onto the boat was dangerous work in rough weather. After this ordeal John came into the cabin, looking very grey, and said, 'That anchor will be the death of me.'

Next day the storm had abated so we decided to go ashore in the dinghy. It was only a short distance to the beach so we didn't put on the outboard, instead John took the oars. He had only rowed a few strokes when he asked me to take over. As soon as we hit the shore, our daughters wanted to climb a large hill nearby. We were all keen except Dad who was suffering from a pain in his chest. A few days later he saw a doctor who told him that he was having difficulty because he wasn't fit. John didn't drink or smoke and he played golf whenever he wasn't boating. Every night before he came home for dinner he would spend two hours at the golf course having practice shots.

I knew something was really wrong when John asked me to help him in the business. He just couldn't cope by himself any more.

Then a bomb shell came; the building that we had worked in for many years was going to be sold. Panic and stress set in. John came to me at work and said that he wasn't feeling well.

I told him to go and lie down in his office. About half an hour later I had a little break, so I went to see how John was getting on. He was unconscious on the floor. We immediately rang for an ambulance and he was taken to hospital. That night the doctor told me that John had had a heart attack and that it was critical. My eldest daughter Gail, who was at a Bible conference, came home and we were all shattered. We got down to some serious praying and asked God to help us. John was spared for another twelve months and recovered enough to go back to work.

With John's ailing health and business worries, our little world was falling apart. We were becoming slaves to the things that had brought us great joy and security in the material world.

It was Easter Thursday and we were on our usual trip to Wellsford (north of Auckland), where we had set up office. Going up the Albany hill, John suddenly called out, 'Quick the brake, the brake!' He bent down and pulled on the brake. His foot was still on the accelerator and the engine roared then stalled. With the van teetering half way up the steep hill, I was terrified that it would start to roll back into the motorists behind. I got out and waved them down and asked them to help me get John out of the van. He was caught in the safety belt but eventually they got him out and laid him in the back of the van. They tried to keep me calm by saying that he was still alive, but I knew he was dead. I got into the van to be with him and covered him with a rug. His eyes were wide open so I closed them and was aware of the presence of God. Christians talk about 'the everlasting arms' and that day I felt God's arms lift me above the situation and fill my body with new strength.

John's funeral service was held at the Soldiers' Memorial Church in Park Road, Titirangi, on Easter Saturday.

When Tuesday came there was no time for grieving. I was at work as usual. Life went on for others and the workers in our business were dependent on me for their livelihood. There was nobody to take over the trip to Wellsford every day, so I did it myself. I did this for over six months and eventually I became so exhausted that I prayed, 'Lord if you want me to do this the rest of my life, I will do it, but if not, will you please sell the business.' At that time it was nearly impossible to sell anything, let alone a manufacturing business, but in a matter of weeks it had sold.

John had often spoken to me about taking the girls on an overseas trip when they finished their studies. So a few months later we left New Zealand on a six week trip to America, England, Scotland, Wales and Europe.

The next Easter my eldest daughter, Gail, was married in the Soldiers' Memorial Church, Titirangi. The Easter after that, my second daughter, Christine, was married in the same church. Within three Easters I found myself alone - but not lonely.

During all these trials and tribulations I was becoming more dependent on God and was constantly being strengthened in my faith.

I served on the session as an elder for twenty years, but the time came when I knew that I had to retire and let someone else take over. This was one of the hardest decisions I've had to make; I felt like I was opting out of God's service. A nasty little voice was saying to me, 'You see you've given all those years in service and now you aren't needed any more.'

Christine, Joyce and Gail at Christine's wedding in 1975

There isn't any unemployment or redundancy in the Christian life and it wasn't long before I realised that the door had now opened into a life of prayer. One day when I settled down to pray, I thought to myself, 'The Lord must be tired of me always asking for things.' So I prayed, 'Lord, I'm not going to ask for anything this morning, I'm just going to praise you.' What a wonderful time I had. The ultimate thing in Christian life is not just service, but to love God, praise his name and enjoy him forever.

Decisions

Life seems to be full of decisions and it's so important to make the right ones.

Our lives are lived out in little worlds that we've created with tinsel and glitter. We have wonderful things to look back on: success in business, sport, marriage, daughters and grandchildren, to name a few. These memories become very important as we grow older. The family has gone and we want to go on living in the past. The past is comfortable. The time comes, because of age or disability, to make a decision.

I was now seventy-two years of age, fit and healthy, but I knew the time was coming when I'd have to move to a smaller house. I'd learned by now that God has a plan for my life, so I took it to him in prayer and asked for his guidance.

A week later, whilst I was driving to get my groceries, I felt a strong persuasion to go and see some new townhouses in Blockhouse Bay, not far from Titirangi, with a view of the sea. There was a man who said he wanted to buy my house when I was ready to leave. So I was able to sell our family home and move to my new town house. The whole change over went smoothly. You can be sure that if you let God into your dec sion-making process, you will make the right choice. When you get an answer to your prayer, don't sit and mull it over - go and check it out.

The latest lesson that I've learned is this: I was prompted that it was now time to share what God had been doing in my life since 1968 when I first wrote 'Part Two' of this book. As I mentioned before, I was hesitant to do this and I started to question God. What will happen to it? Who will want to hear about it? What will it be titled? And the answer came back, 'From Strength to Strength'. Then the words of John 2:1-5 speaking of the wedding feast came to me. The groom's family had run out of wine part way through the celebration. Mary went to Jesus her son and said, 'They have no wine.' I imagined Jesus putting his arm around his mother and saying, 'Why do you involve me? My time has not yet come.'

Mary turned to the servants and simply said, 'Do whatever he tells you to do.'

Jesus asked the servants to fill the water pots with water. The servants were probably puzzled by Jesus' request, but when the water was poured a miracle had taken place - the water had become the highest quality wine. So I have written this knowing that it isn't my business to question God, but to go ahead and do what he's told me to do.

Paul likens the Christian's life to a race. The athlete, once he sets his mind on the prize, will put his body through rigorous training to be strong when the finishing line is in sight.

Perhaps you saw the New Zealand walker at the Commonwealth games in 1998. My heart went out to him. I found myself calling out for him to get up. His race was forty kilometres, he had led most of the way and had only a short distance to go. He looked like a battery toy running out of power. I'm sure that everyone who saw it felt the same as me. It isn't the one who starts out strong, but the one who finishes the race who will win the prize.

The wonderful thing about this athlete was that the next day he was determined to start again.

There's also a new beginning for us. We can go back to the foot of the cross, we can confess to God and ask for his power to start again, so that we will be ready to do whatever he tells us to do.

Two years ago, I woke up at two o'clock in the morning with a racing heart. I was taken to Auckland Hospital and shortly after I arrived a nurse came to check my medical papers.

'There's a mistake here,' she said, 'it says that you were born in 1915. That makes you eighty-two.'

'That's right,' I said.

'You don't look that old. Are you on some sort of a diet?' she asked.

'No,' I said, 'but I have a special person in my life.'

'Oh,' she said, 'who's that?'

'Are you sure you want to know?' I had to ask, because life is never the same after Jesus arrives.

She told me she did want to know, so there I was at three o'clock in the morning talking to her about my encounter with Christ. All those years ago God opened my mouth like Moses and Aaron, but now can't close it!

I'm now eighty-four. His will is good, pleasing and perfect. Heaven is a place of order, love, beauty, peace, security, contentment, joy, laughter and reunion. It is a place where there are no tears, no sickness, no wars and plenty of good things for all.

'Seek first the kingdom of God and his righteousness and all these things will be added to you.' Matthew 6:33.

'But it is written, "Eye has not seen nor ear heard, neither has it entered into the heart of man, the things that God has prepared

for those who love him."' 1 Corinthians 2:9.

When I look back over the years, I can see God's mighty hand leading, teaching and loving. When we accept God's will and plan for our lives we can be sure of a life of adventure and fulfilment.

I have written this book to the glory of God. I'm just an ordinary Kiwi with nothing particularly special about me. I was a woman looking for a new way of life and in searching I found the *way*, the *truth* and the *life* that is Jesus Christ.

I now press on towards 'The Great Prize', God himself, who says,

'Never will I leave you; never will I forsake you.' Hebrews 13:5.

What a friend, what a saviour!